THIS STORY CONTAINS
content that some readers may find
troubling to read relating to sexual
assault, rape, abuse, suicidal thoughts,
self-harm, childhood trauma, alcohol
and drug misuse and PTSD.

Please be mindful of these and other
possible triggers, and seek assistance
if needed.

To the colleagues who became family,
my unquivering pillars of strength
in good times and bad.
To a manager who unknowingly
saved my life.

And to someone who taught me
vulnerability is a strength,
not a weakness,

Thank you.

Chapter One

It was late afternoon, and I was sitting on my bed admiring my new bedroom. Well, the bedroom wasn't new; we had lived in the house for years, but I had recently switched rooms with my sister and had it re-decorated, so it was new to me. I had chosen duck egg and chocolate brown, and although I'll admit at first, I wasn't sure about the combination, I was glad I stuck with those colours. The walls were painted duck egg, the curtains and bedding matched with a mixture of both colours and hints of cream added in here and there. The carpet was a light brown, and everything looked new; you could still smell the paint in the air. My new desk sat in the corner, all shiny and bright, my coloured pens in a metal silver pot just waiting for me to write something fanciful.

My mother walked in. She hadn't knocked, she never did, and handed me the phone. My mother was the sort of parent who snapped easily over the most mundane things, who ruled the home with her 'I'm right, you're wrong' attitude and when questioned by anyone, would fly into an uncontrollable rage. Her outbursts were regular, rarely over important things and she almost never let me or my sister have a choice in anything. She would choose when and which family members we visited and for how long, which school shoes and bags we had for our first day back, how our bedrooms were decorated before we became teenagers, even deciding which clothing and footwear we were allowed to own. We had very little choice growing up. My mother was controlling and rarely smiled or encouraged us. The only time her smile appeared genuine, the kind that starts on your lips and reaches your eyes, was when she was screaming at us. She gained genuine enjoyment from showing us she was boss and what we thought or felt meant nothing to her.

It was my cousin Diane on the phone asking if I wanted to stay overnight for the bank holiday weekend. I had zero plans other than staying in, enjoying my new bedroom, deciding which posters and photos to hang back up.

'Sure, I'd love to' I said, only half meaning it. Don't get me wrong, I loved Diane. We spent a lot of weekends together; we could get along like Disney and happily ever after or like fire and ice. But we did always have fun.

My mum drove me the 20 minutes to Diane's house while Shania Twain's album 'The Woman in Me' played in the car for the 100th time. As soon as we got there, I said hi to my aunt and uncle, bye to my mum and we left to meet up with her friend Kaylee then spent the night doing normal teenage things. We walked around, talked about boys, bitched about our parents, gossiped about friends, wondered what we would be like when we were older, who would be married first and how many kids we each would have. We stopped once we reached a statue where we used black eyeliner and added to all the other writings on it. It was old and in the middle of nowhere but was beginning to look like a real piece of artwork!

After a while, a group of older boys walked up to us. Diane and Kaylee knew them, but I had never met them before. They were older, all dressed in tracksuits, some wearing a baseball cap. I thought this odd as it was dark outside but maybe they didn't have a winters hat or maybe they did but wouldn't be seen dead wearing one with their tracksuits.

'This is my cousin, Lux', Diane offered up. 'And this is Alex', she pointed to one of the boys. His smile sent shivers down my spine, but I politely smiled back. I found out he was a few days away from turning 19, had a car, had finished school, and was looking for a job. None of the others were introduced to me. The date was Friday 18th February 2000.

The boys asked if we wanted to join them in going to one of the other's houses. 'We're just going to hang out and listen to music', Alex explained. Diane and Kaylee practically skipped with elation at being invited. I myself was not overly zealous at this thought and cautiously trailed behind.

The bedroom smelled of cigarettes and weed, I felt nauseated as soon as we sat down. The guys spent their time joking with each other, usually at the expense of their friends in the room. It was easy to acknowledge from listening to them, that they had a strong bond, one which had been formed throughout years of friendship. When we sat down on the unmade, unmatched bed, the guys rapidly got to rolling joints—something I had never actually seen done before and was initially intrigued by. Someone declared, 'Take a draw', and held it under my nose. My face surely was a picture because everyone laughed out loud in sync, and it was swiftly passed to Diane and Kaylee, who acted like this was not the first time they were trying it.

Once that was finished, two of them rummaged in the bottom of an old, busted wardrobe coming out with what I could only describe as a 2ltr bottle of juice that had been manually besieged. It was cut in half and filled with what appeared to be water. Inside was a broken glass bottle, the lid had holes poked in it, the 'green' was put into the lid of the glass bottle, which was then burned with a lighter. It filled with smoke, the glass bottle was pulled up, and the smoke quickly inhaled. Again, I was asked if I 'Wanted a go', but politely declined. The guys appeared harmless and I never once felt forced to try anything. They made us laugh, played some rave music, then walked us all home.

The following day my aunt dragged us into town. Normally, Diane and I would have enjoyed this; however, we spent most of the time sitting on the dressing room floor of M&S while my aunt tried on outfit after outfit and sent us to get things in different sizes.

As we sat, I found myself studying the vast number of mannequins around us, all dressed in different outfits, all with the same expressionless look upon their faces. There was one, dressed in a chequered brown and tan skirt, a burnt orange polo-neck jumper with brown knee-high boots that stood in a boxed window staring down at the busy street below, a look of sadness on its face. I wondered what it would think or say if it were real, would it hold everyone's secrets or scream them out loud to passers-by. Needless to say, by the end of the shopping trip, Diane and I were disinterested and exhausted when we boarded the train.

We were craving food by the time we arrived home, and after a long day of playing fashion show assistants, my uncle treated us all to dinner at a pizza place. We loved the pizza place. Diane and I would order the smallest pizza we could find on the menu then fill up on bowl after bowl of whippy ice cream. We would take turns seeing who could fit the most sweets into their bowl, and by the time we were in the car heading home, we were fit to burst.

'It's still early, can we go to Kaylee's?' Diane cautiously asked her parents, stealing a glance at me.

'I think it would be better if you girls got into your pyjamas and had a movie night at home', my uncle told us. I had been coughing and sneezing all day and had a throbbing headache, but I knew Kaylee's parents were having friends over for a party which meant she would allow us to have a few bottles of Hooch or Smirnoff Ice to share.

Changing into my PJ's, curling up on the couch, and watching a movie sounded wonderful, but I knew how much Diane wanted to go to Kaylee's, so I compiled all the energy I had left and smiled.

'I'm feeling much better after dinner, and going to Kaylee's will be fun', I lied. My uncle agreed he would call Kaylee's mum when we got home to make sure it was okay if we visited. He had no idea she was having a party, and she would never have told him this as she knew how strict Diane's parents were, and they would disapprove of us being there around adults who were drinking. My uncle stayed true to his word and called Kaylee's mum as soon as he walked through the front door, who related she would be delighted to have us come over.

The walk to Kaylee's house was fresh. It was winter, the air smelled crisp and clear, and the ground was covered in ice crystals. It was the first time that day I felt I could take a deep breath and have my lungs fill up without feeling like they were on fire. It was that time of year that inspired the wearing of layers. We were wrapped up warm in our coats, gloves, and a scarf but had both refused to wear a hat as it would mess up the hair we had spent 20 minutes styling before we left.

We arrived 15 minutes later and were greeted at the front door by Kaylee and her mum, who swiftly ushered us into the kitchen and related we could take any of the little bottles but not to touch the spirits. Kaylee's mum filled some white plastic bowls with crisps and nuts, and we headed upstairs. I was not a big underage drinker at that point; I had tasted alcohol before at different parties, but I had too many older cousins who I had witnessed get in trouble with alcohol, and I wouldn't say I liked getting into trouble. I was a good girl who would rarely succumb to peer pressure and I was proud of that.

Diane and Kaylee headed upstairs to the bedroom as I sluggishly followed at their feet. The bedroom was a warm and inviting space. It was bubble-gum pink with teen magazine posters showing her favourite bands – 911, Boyzone and Backstreet Boys covering most of the walls, CD's laying out messy in the corner by the door and heart shaped fluffy pink and white throw pillows scattering the floor among dirty clothes and old trainers. Kaylee had a white canopy bed with baby-pink fabric draped over the top and on all sides. A white wardrobe and dresser sat together at the bottom of her bed and a make-up table stood perched under the window, camouflaged in perfume bottles, schoolbooks, nail polishes and costume jewellery. The smell of perfume and hairspray lingered in the air as the stereo blared with songs from the latest top charts.

We sat in Kaylee's bedroom, her and Diane sitting on the floor with their legs crossed listening to music, talking about school and boys, while I lay on the bed and prayed for my cold to vanish. After a while, I gave up trying to overcome my sickness and declared I was going home.

'If you go, I have to go too, and I want to stay', Diane firmly told me, her forehead wrinkled as her eyebrows were brought together in a scowl.

'Just sleep in my bed, and we'll wake you when it's time to go home', pleaded Kaylee. I sighed, laying back down on the soft bed with clean silky sheets for a while and closed my eyes. It didn't take long before the sound of the party downstairs, the girlie laughter coming from Diane and Kaylee, and the stickly heat in the bedroom became too much for my increasing headache to handle.

'I'm going home. I'll tell your mum and dad you both walked me to the roundabout and came back here' I declared matter-of-factly to them both.

'Fine, you better not tell them we've been drinking, or I'll tell them you were too', threatened Diane. She could be so immature at times. I wrapped up tight in my layers to fight against the cold, and I left. I remember looking at my stainless steel Sekonda watch; it had two silver bands that twisted on either end coming together with a simple clasp to hold it in place. The time was just after 7:30 pm. Little did I know my stubbornness that night was about to change my whole life.

Chapter Two

My drinking commenced the Tuesday following that cataclysmic night. I remember standing in the kitchen waiting on my sister so we could leave for school together. I'm not sure why we had to do this because as soon as the garden gate was closed, she met up with her friends, I met up with mine, and we pretended not to know of each other's existence until we walked back through that same gate after school.

Anyway, here I was patiently waiting in the kitchen for her on this wintery February morning, layers covering the marks he had left on my body 3 days prior, still feeling stiff and sore, when I noticed one of the cupboard doors was slightly ajar. I liked things in my life to be neat and organized, so I walked over and began closing it. It was at this point I noticed the alcohol inside it. It wasn't that I didn't know the alcohol was there; it was more I had never really thought about it before. I stood there staring at the different bottles for what seemed like hours but could only have been a few minutes.

Before my mind could catch up with the rest of my body, I was opening the fridge, taking out a bottle of diet coke, pouring roughly half down the sink before adding vodka to it and quickly throwing this into my school bag.

Each day I would continue this, it quickly becoming part of my morning routine. I would start with vodka, when that ran low I would add Bacardi, then gin, and eventually whiskey. When the contents of all bottles were running low, I would make my own special cocktail by adding a little of each to the one bottle of diet coke and hiding this in my school bag before topping the bottles up with water. The cocktails tasted horrible, but I quickly learned if you used coke instead of diet coke, it didn't taste as bad.

About a month after I started drinking in school, I became friends with a girl in my year named Gaby. She was going through a hard time, and I knew exactly what it felt like to be dealing with something and have to paint a happy face on in front of everyone else. It was exhausting.

At this point, I had started drinking almost daily, and when I shared this with Gaby, she was only too happy to join me in my new distraction technique and numb her pain too. I would meet Gaby before school, we would share the full bottle before the bell rang, be drunk for registration, and by lunch, the buzz would have worn off. This is when I would make up two bottles of my special cocktail so we could keep the buzz lasting until the last school bell rang.

My parents had people over at least once a month, so the reduction in alcohol wasn't noticed. When they had a party, I would play the favourable daughter always pouring the drinks then tidying up once everyone left. I would take the bottles that had a little left in them, add them all to one bottle, hide this in my bedroom, then tidy the rest away,. My parents would think someone at the party had finished the alcohol and there were never any questions asked. It was that easy.

I started standing with the older kids at lunch where I would partake in smoking a joint or taking any pills they had; I didn't ask what they were, and I survived my days.

I had prided myself on being a good student and school had always been so effortless to me. I loved learning things, and if I didn't know something, I was never afraid of asking. My teachers had always told me, 'If you don't understand something, just ask. It's better to ask and know the answer than to sit and struggle'.

And that's exactly what I did. I was never cocky when it came to schoolwork, and I would help explain any problem or solution to my classmates when they asked. And they did ask. I enjoyed school, I loved learning all about different subjects in the same day.

I would participate in group discussions, demonstrate during art, take the lead when asked to during music, and I even loved PE. This eagerness to learn and soak up everything new started from Primary 1 and followed me right through to my Third Year at High School.

Before my Third Year, I never drank alcohol or stood smoking with my classmates at lunchtime. My homework was always done on time, and I continued to enjoy learning new things, approaching new challenges head-on.

In the few weeks which followed that night, I had stopped doing my homework or I would start it and not finish. Or my teachers would see me doing it before school or during breaks and tell me it was called homework for a reason. I was either loud and had an opinion on everything, thanks to the courage of my cocktails, or I was silent and wouldn't speak during class, thanks to the hangovers my cocktails left me with.

I was rude to everyone. I wasn't the same me, I was the new me. Most of my teachers noticed the vast difference in my behaviour and would hold me back after class to ask what was wrong.

'Somethings wrong, I can see it. You've changed. You can talk to me', they would say. The more they said the same things, the more pissed off I got. I knew I had changed; I knew I was different but I didn't care, and I was not about to have a heart-to-heart with any of my teachers about it as they would race directly to my parents if they knew the truth.

I started going to underage dancing parties with friends from school. There was strictly no alcohol served, but that did not mean no alcohol was drank. They never searched us. We would go in; order fizzy juice and a glass of ice, then add our poison of the week which we carried in under our coats.

I noticed it was taking more and more for me to feel like I had been drinking. I just wasn't capturing the same buzz as quickly as I had before, so I would drink a bottle of my own specially made cocktail before I went out. I was much better company when I was drunk anyway; I felt free, I didn't care who saw me or what I did and drinking gave me the only escape from the horrors going on in my life. It was draining to be on high alert every second of the day.

I never reached the point where I was black-out drunk. I always knew where I was, always watched my surroundings, spotted the exits as soon as I walked into anywhere new, and I knew exactly where my friends were at all times. But I did have fun at the same time, or so I thought. Looking back now I understand I was trying to numb the never-ending ache I felt within myself.

Before that night, I was never impolite to anyone; that just wasn't who I was. But when my teachers repeatedly asked me the same questions, when they became impatient with me continuously trying to convince them I was fine, when they appeared sincere at first then transform, standing in front of me demanding I tell them what was wrong, then my defence-mechanism kicked in and I became mad. I had to protect myself and my secrets at all costs or he would hunt me down and make me pay for talking. I wanted to tell someone what was going on, what he had done to me that night, what had happened since, but I was more afraid of him than my own demons that were beginning to surface so I remained silent. He told me no-one would believe me anyway, so why bother trying.

I would shout at my teachers; I would tell them they were all crazy and there to teach me, not harass me. Some were easier to get around than others, some would ask once or twice before giving up on me, but others would continually come at me with their line of questioning. I would eventually stop talking, standing there in silence staring at the ground waiting for them to get bored and tell me I could leave. 'Stay still, don't look them in the eye and you'll be safe. He'll ask again if you've told anyone and if you lie he'll know and kill you just as he promised' I would remind myself. My life had quickly became a nightmare, but I didn't want to die.

I remember this one day, maybe 3 months after that fateful night. It was last period, and I was sitting in Geography looking out the window at the dark grey clouds rolling in when someone from another class entered with a note for my teacher. She read it, casually walked over to me, and whispered that a PE teacher wanted to see me after class. I immediately responded, 'Why? I'm not going! She can't keep me here after the bell rings'.

My teacher explained, 'When a teacher asks to see you, you can't say no'. Well, this enraged me further. Why did she want to see me? Mrs. Henderson wasn't even my regular PE teacher! I hadn't seen her that day. It had been a few days since I was last in PE, so what could she possibly want to see me about? She had never taken much interest in me before, so what's changed now?

I'm not sure if it was the rage in me that needed an outlet, and a fight with a teacher would do just that, or if curiosity got the better of me, but I calmed down enough by the end of class before making my way downstairs to the PE department.

Mrs. Henderson was in the office when I arrived. I quietly knocked on the door, and a male teacher told me to come in. Mrs. Henderson smiled at me and took me into the deserted corridor.

She asked how my day had gone. 'Fine, what do you want'? I snapped. She appeared very calm, her smile warm as my gaze caught hers.

'I just wanted you to know that I'm here if you ever need someone to talk with'. That was it. That was all she said as she put a reassuring hand on my shoulder. I stood there in silent shock for a few seconds before turning and walking away.

Little did she know, I stood at the end of that corridor for 20 minutes and couldn't take another step. My heart wanted to run back and tell Mrs. Henderson everything, every single little detail I could remember. It were as though I had a burning ball inside me, inside my stomach, inside my chest, and all I had to do was open my mouth to release it, but I couldn't. The voice in my head took over every time.

'They'll call your parents. They won't believe you. He told you if you ever opened your mouth it would be the last thing you ever did. Do you want to die'? These thoughts took over my body, snuffed out the fire inside me, and allowed my legs to run in the opposite direction, again.

I rarely took part in PE. My teachers all used to it by now and having long given up on asking me to join my classmates. I refused to wear shorts and a t-shirt because I always had cuts and bruises and different marks covering my body. How would I explain them? There were only so many times you could fall down or walk into something. I had broken my wrists three times during the year and a half since that night and was quickly running out of believable excuses.

Well, I didn't break them; they were broken for me. My left wrist once and my right wrist twice. I'm right-handed and had to quickly become good at writing with my left hand, which I surprised myself by being quite good at. I refused to be in an office using a helper who would write for me when sitting my prelims and struggled through completing all my exams on my own with a broken wrist. The pain at the end of each exam was excruciating but it was easier than explaining why I had yet another broken bone.

I remember my maths teacher becoming increasingly angry at me once because I sat in her classroom one afternoon and refused to take my black school jumper off. It was so warm, and everyone else was sitting in their white polo shirts, ties removed while all the windows in the classroom were open. It was last period and I just wanted to survive the class and be done with school for the day.

'Lux, do you have special ice packs built into your jumper that the rest of us don't'? She stood in front of the class and asked, the other students all laughing at her. Or were they laughing at me? The more I refused to remove my jumper, the more frustrated she became until she was standing at my desk demanding I remove it.

I was used to teachers becoming angry with me by now, so I ignored her, instead continuing to work on the maths problem she had put up on the board. She kept me behind that day and, for the 100th time, asked me what was wrong.

'Roll your sleeves up; I want to check something' she demanded.

'Hell no'. I said to myself. God himself could have come down and demanded the very same; however, that would never happen. The reason being, I had a bad cut on my left lower arm and had been using wet paper towels in the hope of stopping the bleeding from soaking through my jumper. She eventually gave up, as they all did, and let me leave.

During lunch, my friends and I would sit in an empty classroom. My best friend had repeatedly asked me for the last few months what was wrong but I would easily brush her off by saying some guy had tried to kiss me, but I had pushed him off, and he didn't like it. However, on this day, she kept pushing me all through lunch break until I had finally had enough. I stared at the table. 'She's your best friend, you're supposed to tell each other everything. She'll believe you' I reminded myself.

'I told you someone tried to kiss me, and I pushed him away, but that wasn't the whole truth'. I explained very briefly and in as little detail as possible the events that occurred that night. We sat together in complete silence until the bell rang then we stood up; I went to one class, and she another.

We had maths last period together, but she didn't show up at the start of class. I stood frozen in fear as I heard my fellow classmate inform our teacher how my friend had been extremely upset during last period and was talking with her teacher in the office. I thought, 'This is it; my secret is out. My life is over'.

But it wasn't. She didn't disclose what I had told her, and to this day, we have never discussed it. I thought if my best friend couldn't handle knowing it, I would never tell another living soul ever again. I could not have anyone upset because of me.

Chapter Three

In Fourth Year, my maths teacher was not someone you could brush off or easily ignore. One afternoon, I casually walked into her classroom and realised I had left my glasses in my previous class. 'Great' I sighed. It was last period and my body ached from a few short blows I had received 3 days before from Alex. All I wanted to do was go home, take a bath and be done with the day but no, because of my own carelessness I now had to walk all the way to the other side of the school and collect my glasses before walking all the way back. I stood up and nonchalantly told my teacher I had to go collect them.

'You know, you should be more careful' she replied. This was not said with any malice, she was just letting me know that I should be more careful with important things such as my glasses. Well, I did not take this so kindly.

I had to be more careful? How dare she! Didn't she know my whole life now revolved around me being careful? I had to be careful with my behaviour and not let too much away. I had to be careful in covering up my skin to hide the cuts and bruises. I had to be careful with how much alcohol I drank each day so my parents wouldn't find out it was missing, and my teachers wouldn't suspect I had been drinking during school. I had to be careful when getting in and out of bed because sometimes the beatings were just too damn painful and getting out of bed quickly could set me up for a day of more pain that I then had to summon the strength to mask. I had to be careful not to let anything slip or he would inflict more pain on me. I had to be careful to act as normally as I possibly could around friends and family. I had to be careful when taking a shower whenever I had a fresh wound as the soap would cause it to sting and allow tears to momentarily escape from my eyes and slide down my cheeks. I had to be careful with my emotions around him as I didn't want to show any weakness. I had to be careful not to scream too loudly whenever my body and soul were being used as punching bags. I had to be careful in doing exactly what he told me to do, exactly how he told me to it; otherwise, I would be punished further.

I had to be careful every single damn day of my whole damn life, and on the large scale of things, leaving my glasses in another classroom did not marginally come close to something I cared about being careful with. Didn't she know my life, my whole existence, now depended on me being careful? No, she didn't. How could she when I never told anyone.

'Don't you tell me what to do! You're here to teach maths! That's all! So, stick to that!' I roared at her in front of everyone. I left the classroom, slamming the door closed behind me, and went to retrieve my glasses. I furiously walked the long corridors to my previous class, gaining no enjoyment from the fire doors that refused to slam shut even when I pushed with all my might. The walls were cream, marked carelessly with holes from years of posters, scuff marks from shoes and school bags and every so often you would find a small drawing, barely a few centimetres in size, sitting on the skirting boards, watching us, judging us as we hurried past.

As I entered my previous class, the teacher had already starting her lesson. I told her why I was there and went to look for my glasses but couldn't find them. She came over and asked the 4 students at the long desk to stand up and help us. They slowly stood, stealing glances at each other and pulled their chairs out as I crouched down to look on the floor. Still nothing. The teacher had seen me wearing them so knew they must be somewhere and asked the younger students if they had been there when they took their seat. No answer. She asked again but no-one spoke. She had the students lift their bags and jackets and stand in the middle of the class while she searched the area. Once she was fully satisfied they were not where I had left them, she turned to the students and appealed for the truth. She told them she knew they were lying and demanded someone speak up. One of the boys slowly reached into his pocket and pulled out my glasses. The lenses had been smashed and the frame was bent in several places. She started yelling at them, wanting to know who had done this but I didn't care who or why. I snatched them out of the boys' hand and left.

When I returned to class, my teacher was standing in the corridor waiting on me with an apprehensive look on her face. The classroom door was closed and as I went to walk in she put her arm out in front of me, blocking my way.

'If you want me to spend your class standing outside in the corridor then that's fine with me' I again snapped at her.

She shook her head. 'You have two choices Lux; you can stay after class and talk with me, or you can stay after class and talk with your guidance counsellor. But you *are* staying after class and talking with one of us because we *are* getting to the bottom of this today' she stiffly told me, a stern look upon her face.

I was marginally entertained for a moment by her will to break mine. I knew my guidance counsellor was easy to get around, and after finding my broken glasses I was in the mood for a good challenge, so I stood tall, chest puffed out, stared her square in the eyes and countered with, 'You'll do', as I sarcastically smiled, rolled my eyes at her laughable proclamation before heading into class. I could feel my peers' eyes on me as I took my seat but I was unbothered by this.

I do vividly recall that class. I was laughing, normally and not sarcastically for a change, something I had not done in almost a year. I remember for the first time in a long time, enjoying learning again. I listened to what was being said, I voluntarily answered question without having to be asked first and I completed my work just like every other student there. I even took note of my homework and was almost certain I would complete this on time for once. Was I becoming myself again? Were my behaviours and attitude finally changing for the better? Or was I just having fun before my big head-to-head with my teacher?

Our classroom was a peaceful, fun place to learn. It allowed us to have self-confidence, taught us to have respect for authority and also be brave enough to question that authority when needed. I had always loved learning. I had loved a lot of things, before.

When the bell rang, I had a momentarily lapse in memory about being summoned to stay behind, that was until I headed for the door and heard 'Lux, you wait right there', coming from my teachers' desk in the corner of the room.

'Oh yeah, it's fight time again', the voice in my head eagerly reminded me and I smiled.

She waited until everyone else left then slowly closed the door as I took a seat at the front of the class. It was one of those single square desks that were more common in American schools on TV than in my school. You could see where the pen marks had almost been fully erased from the top of the table. 'If only it were that simple to erase things', I cited quietly to myself.

My teacher stood in front of me wearing a green A-line skirt and matching jumper with her arms folded across her chest. And she smelled of coffee. Not in a bad way, she was just always drinking it and often had a mug sitting on her desk. 'Had she always been so tall'? I thought quietly to myself. As I sat there, I could feel the power of her stare trying to pierce my very soul, and I swiftly decided it better not to hold eye contact with her. If I didn't look at her, she couldn't break me.

'What's going on? I know there's something. Please don't tell me it's nothing. I'm worried about you', she sought for my truth.

'I'm fine', I lied, again. I was getting good at this lying game. These days I wore my lies like armour.

'You are not fine. You look like you're about to pass out'.

'I don't know what everyone's problem is with me, and I'm getting a little sick and tired of playing this game over and over again' I added as I sat back in the chair and folded my arms to mirror hers, still thinking it best not to look directly at her.

But she was having none of it. 'You are not fine. You stare blankly in class like you are in another world. Your mood is low. Your whole personality has changed Lux. I cannot remember the last time I genuinely saw you smile or heard your laugh. You were always smiling; I could hear your laugher before you stepped into my classroom. Your friends are worried about you, they tell me you're not eating and they feel like you are giving up on yourself. All your teachers are worried too', she continued to search for answers.

She pulled a chair around and sat in front of me at this tiny desk. Just as I had predicted, she wasn't giving up easily. I had always liked this teacher, she was fun, could relate to us teenagers, and was just one of those adults you felt you could talk to. She didn't treat us like we were kids.

I slowly lifted my gaze to match hers and saw a genuine look of worry upon her face, her eyebrows were pulled up together, her mouth stretched and drawn back. She didn't look angry, as though speaking with me was a chore for her but instead, she looked as though she cared. Unlike the teachers before her who usually looked more annoyed than anything else to have to be dealing with my new found attitude.

In that moment, I made a terrifying decision. I couldn't tell her my whole truth, but maybe I could tell her something, you know, 'test the waters' and see what her reaction would be. 'There was this guy a while ago, he tried to kiss me and wanted me to have sex with him, but I didn't want to, so I pushed him off and he didn't like that', I cautiously explained.

'So, he tried to kiss you and asked you to have sex; you told him no and pushed him away'? She slowly repeated.

'Yes'. I waited with bated breath for her response. 'Please understand what I'm not telling you' I silently pleaded.

'And did anything else happen Lux'?

'No' I lied to her. 'Yes, please help me, I'm drowning' the voice in my head screamed. 'She said she were worried, she's noticed how much I've changed, surely she won't easily give up on me too'.

'So, if nothing happened, then there's nothing to worry about, is there? Lux, you cannot walk around acting like this over something that nearly, but did not actually happen', she firmly told me. 'If you are having trouble dealing with it then write it down', she suggested. 'Oh yeah, like writing anything down could solve my current problems', I thought to myself.

I had always held tremendous respect for this teacher; she had kind eyes, would find a new way to explain something if we struggled to understand the problem and she treated us like young adults rather than children. She never seemed bothered by us like so many others and she made learning fun. She was also disciplined and strict, all of these attributes together were what made me highly respect her. She understood perfectly that setting the right environment in class was the key to her students learning with ease, however, as I sat across from her, that respect swiftly evaporated into thin air. She did hand me a blank jotter to write in though. Up went my walls, and on went my body armour, again. 'How could I have been so wrong about her'? I cried to myself as I walked home.

As soon as I got there, I headed straight upstairs, tore open my schoolbag, rummaged for that jotter and furiously threw it onto the pile of old schoolwork laying on my desk. I didn't want it in my bag for a second longer, infecting my other ones with its blank pages and crisp new cover. I was angry, I was hurting and I was now of the firm belief that no-one could ever help me. I was all alone.

I could feel it sitting there though, glaring at me, daring me to open it each time I sat down at the desk, but I ignored it every time. It sat there, part of a pile of books for a few weeks until I was clearing out my desk one rainy Sunday afternoon. I cleared all around the jotter and the pile it had become accustomed to sitting in. I got a spray and cloth and cleaned every inch around the pile, then when everything else was squeaky clean and smelling fresh, I lifted this forgotten pile of books. I didn't dare touch that jotter though. I threw them onto my bed before setting about cleaning the rest of my desk then carefully I placed my things back where they had been.

When I finally got to the jotter, I dared hold it in my hands. There was nothing physically scary about it, but the pages being filled with everything that my head was holding, that was a terrifying thought. It wasn't the blank jotter that filled me with anxiety and fear, but rather what it could become.

Over time, fear and I developed a strong admiration for one another. The feeling of being afraid was keeping me alert every single day. It was keeping me awake when all I wanted to do was fall asleep, it was keeping the blood in my veins pumping and it was keeping me on high alert for any dangers around me. In effect, it was keeping me alive and had become like a security blanket that I could wrap myself in and feel protected by. If I was afraid I would see dangers coming, I could protect myself better.

As I lifted the blank jotter, I could feel my new friend fear start to awaken in the pit of my stomach. I closed my eyes and delicately held it in my hands for a few moments. I was fighting an internal battle between getting down in paper what was holding my brain and heart captive, against feeling like at any moment I could explode into a fit of rage and tears and cause real harm to myself, or worse, to someone else.

I quietly sat down at my desk, took out a new packet of pens, opened the front cover and nervously started to write. My teachers voice echoing in my head "If you're having trouble dealing with it then write it down". And that's exactly what I did. I wrote down everything I could remember about that night, every single miniscule detail. I finished it by writing 'I'm scared my mum and dad will find out. How do you explain to them that this awful thing happened to their daughter and not have them blame themselves'? I wrote of nothing that had happened since that night, and when I was done, I closed the jotter and hid it at the bottom of a junk drawer in my bedroom.

A few weeks after doing this, I arrived home from the cinema one night and found my mum sitting on my bed. She looked angry as she told me to close the door and sit down. She was clutching the jotter in her hands.

"What's this"? she questioned, her eyes narrowing. My mouth jumped open and words were coming out faster than my brain could comprehend what was going on.

'Something happened one night, it wasn't a big deal but I didn't like it and someone at school told me to write it down like a story and make it worse so I would realise what actually happened really wasn't that bad after all'. My brain has never worked as hard or as fast as it did in those few seconds. The words had flown out of my mouth so rapidly and with such ease.

The story was sheer gibberish. No normal person would have ever believed it. I searched her eyes and face for any sign of emotion that could heed me to what would happen next, but I saw nothing. Her face was stone, and her eyes were dark. She slowly stood up, glared at me with a look of repulsion, thrust the jobber onto my bed and bitterly told me "Bin it" before turning on her heels and ferociously walking out of my bedroom. To this day it has never been brought up in conversation.

I sat there in disbelief. Half of me was relieved I did not have to go into any detail but the other half of me was angry. The story was bullshit! Anyone else could have seen that! Why didn't she question it? Why had she taken what I said then as truth when she had *word for word* in her hands of what happened, and she walks out on me? This was after she had been called to the school by three teachers over a two-year period, telling her they were worried about me, that they thought I had been drinking during school, that my friends had raised their concerns with them as I had stopped eating, that I hadn't fully completed a piece of homework in months. All of this and she looks at me with repulsion and just walks out? She was my mother, the one person in the world who is supposed to support, protect, and love you and she just walks away? I knew in that very moment I would never tell anyone what had or what was continuing to happen.

Chapter Four

I left Kaylee's house that wintery Saturday night and started on my journey home. It was dark, icy, and bitterly cold. I remember clearly how my toes felt numb in my boots and I were shivering, the cold oozing its way in and chilling my bones, almost freezing my blood.

As I walked along the desolate road, I saw a figure begin to materialise up ahead. There were no streetlights on this patch of road which made it difficult to conclude who the figure was as he waved at me. As he became closer, I recognised it was one of the guys from the night before. 'What was his name again'? I asked myself.

'Alright, you're Diane and Kaylee's mate from last night' he stated rather than asked. 'I'm Alex remember'? 'Where's Diane and Kaylee'? He enquired.

'They're at Kaylee's house, I'm heading home' I casually answered. For a second I felt safer having an older guy with me, the road was eerily quiet, especially dark and I hated to admit it, but I was a little fearful of being out on my own. Alex saw me shiver and asked if I wanted to wear his white Fred Perry jumper. I was wrapped up in many layers and he was wearing a jumper with a t-shirt underneath, nothing else. I smiled politely, declined his offer, and told him I better be going. I was beginning to get a bad vide from the way he stood stared at me like a piece of meat and quickly wanted to be far away from him.

'It's not safe to walk alone out here, what if a car hit black ice and ran into you, nobody would know you were there' Alex responded.

'I'll be fine, it's not a far walk' I replied. 'Although he did have a point' I thought quietly to myself and pushed the uneasy feeling to the back of my mind. If Diane and Kaylee trusted him, then I should too.

We began walking as he slipped his right arm around my shoulders, pulling me close. I thought he must be cold wearing such few layers in this wintery cold so I didn't attempt to shrug him off. I wasn't comfortable with him walking by myside, but I hadn't know him well enough to tell him no, and I had a distinct feeling I did not want to make him angry; especially when I was all alone.

He pulled a bottle of alcohol from his back pocket, took a large gulp, and asked me if I wanted some; I shook my head. He slipped the bottle back into his pocket and light a joint, the smoke catching my throat and causing me to cough. If I close my eyes I can still smell the mixture of smoke along with his Cool Waters aftershave making me queasy.

'I know what will help with that cough' he laughed as he pulled my face towards his and hastily kissed my lips. He were at least six feet tall and had to bend down causing him to stumble in his drunken state. I caught him, making sure he were steady before pushing him away. He stood tall; laughing, with both hands in the air telling me he were sorry; but I ignored him and continued walking away. I wasn't afraid of him now, I just thought he were a creep.

He rapidly caught up with me, slipped his arm back across my shoulders and again, pulled me close. 'He's harmless' I told myself. 'Just walk quickly and you'll be home'.

'I need to pee' he informed me as we were coming to the end of the road. I thought this meant he had to go home and reiterated I was fine to walk the remainder of the way on my own; however, he smirked and told me he wasn't going home. He again apologised for kissing me and asked me to cross the road with him, standing guard in case any cars passed while he walked into the field to relieve himself. There hadn't been a single car pass us yet, so I shook my head no.

'Come on, it'll only take a second. I've already been arrested and if I get caught pissing outside they'll lock me up and throw away the key' he casually laughed. 'A little dramatic' I said to myself. All I had to do was cross the road for a few minutes, then it wouldn't matter if we continued walking as when you reached the end of the road and turned, there were homes on either side and the area was very well lit. 'It'll take two minutes' I reasoned with myself as I rolled my eyes, not wanting to cross the road with him.

He smiled, took a step towards me and taking my left wrist, started to pull me across the road. It wasn't a firm pull, just enough to start me walking. I allowed him to guide me; not trying to anger him. We crossed the road to a patch of grass that looked deathly black having the moonlight be the only thing lighting our way. He didn't let go of my wrist and I asked him what he was doing.

'We need to walk further in so no-one sees' he explained as though I were a child. We had been swallowed up whole by the darkness but we kept walking, his grip still tight around my wrist. The ground was hard beneath our feet which I found strange as we were walking across a field of grass that was usually soft and squishy. Even though he had my wrist, he was walking ahead as I followed behind. I could see his large frame from the back, tall and toned, the jumper slightly tight around his muscles.

He had briefly mentioned the night before how he trained as a boxer for a few years but had to give it up after an injury in the ring. Watching from behind, I could see how powerful he still looked.

I heard him pull the bottle from his back pocket again. It was strange looking; dark blue and green, square in shape and almost flat, more like a hip flask than a bottle. The label was written in a foreign language and I could only presume someone had brought it back as a souvenir for him. As he slipped this into his pocket, all I could hear was the crunching of frozen earth below our feet and the little alcohol that were left swishing around with each step he took.

I turned around, looking at how far we had walked from the road, when I felt him pull me down. I instantly thought I made him lose his balance by turning around and tried to jump up to help him, but he climbed on top of me and I couldn't move. It was as this exact moment I began to feel afraid.

He sat straddling me, both hands around my neck, his face so close to mine I couldn't tell whose breath was whose. I could feel his eyes burning into me but it was too dark to see. He easily pulled my scarf from my neck and threw it onto the ground then unzipped my jacket as his hand glided down my body. He slipped his icy hand under my jumper and t-shirt and held it there against my stomach. That jumper was one of my favourites. My aunt had bought it for me at Christmas, it was multi-coloured, bright, soft and 2 sizes too big, just the way I liked my jumpers. I never wore it again after that night.

I tried to push him off but he was a dead weight. I tried to kick but my legs couldn't move as he pinned them down. I used my fists to hit out but it were as though I were hitting him with feathers, he didn't even flinch. I tried to turn over, pushing myself up onto my elbows as he grabbed both hands in unison and held them above my head with one hand, using the other to punch me, hard, in the face.

He punched at my shoulders, my arms, my stomach. I tried to scream but no sound came out as he clenched his hand tight around my neck. He always went for my neck; every time I saw him he instinctively went for my neck. I hate things touching my neck now, scarfs, necklaces, clothing. I can barely wear my hair down as the feeling causing memories to flood my thoughts and makes it hard to breathe.

'Please don't! Please stop! No!' I cried out as his grip loosened, but my words fell on deaf ears.

As he held his hand steady against my skin, I noticed how cold it was when the one around my neck felt warm. Was this such a strange thought to be having at this moment? His hand was removed from my stomach as I heard a thud and idiotically thought someone had seen us and was coming to my rescue but it had only been the glass bottle falling from his back pocket as he unzipped his jeans and hastily pulled them down. 'What is he doing'? I childishly wondered to myself, unaware of the horror that was coming next.

He pulled at my jeans and the button came undone so easily. He didn't struggle with it, it just popped open. He moved his hand to my zip and pulled this down, again with such ease. My brain became besieged with fear as realisation hit. But wasn't this something adults did? Was I now about to become an adult? I didn't feel like one. Surely I was supposed to be older before I had sex for the first time?

I became unable to think, unable to move as he laughed out loud and bent down to kiss me on the lips. The following few seconds are a blur. I can't recall the exacts moments, however, the pain of him inside me is something I will never forget. I gasped as the air suddenly became thick and almost too difficult to enter my lungs. He was like a hunter, greedy and confined to his own wants and cravings, thinking of me only as something to be used to fulfil his ego and not as the person I was. I know the word that describes what he did to me that night, but I dare let it escape my lips.

I closed my eyes but instantaneously opened them. I didn't want to feel him, I didn't want to see him but if I could just find something else to concentrate on until he finished then I would be okay. I told myself if I could just think, concentrate on something else, anything else then I would be okay. My eyes had become acquainted to the darkness by now and I fiercely looked around for something to focus on. There were no trees, no flowers, no stones, no litter, just the half empty bottle that had fallen from his pocket. I stared at it, thinking how it looked like the ocean had been captured inside as the liquid swayed back and forth and crashed against the glass sides.

I have no idea how long it went on, it felt like hours but could only have been a few minutes. When he was finished he kissed my neck, pulled at my bra one last time, and sat up, legs still straddling me, him still deep inside me. I remembered this video we had been shown in school about having sex for the first time and how it could hurt so I wasn't surprised by the presence of pain. A little confused as I hadn't realised it would be as painful as it had been, but I still thought it normal. 'The video should have made this clearer' I concluded to myself.

As he stood up, I felt him exit me. It was such a strange sensation and I wondered how I hadn't felt him enter. 'Surely I would have felt that' I thought to myself. As he stood, he told me to zip myself up then pulled me by my jumper to my feet. He bent down and picked up the bottle, opening it to take a drink then offering it to me. When I didn't respond he grabbed my face in his hand, forced my mouth open and poured the burning liquid down my throat. He laughed as I choked on it, asking me if I wanted more as I shook my head no.

'That's because you're a good girl' he pulled me close and whispered in my ear. 'My sweet princess'. It sent lightening shivers through my spine. He pushed me to walk and I did. I was surprised at how easily I moved; I could feel no pain. 'Had I not tried strongly enough to get away? Should I have kicked, punched, fought harder to escape? Surely I hadn't fought as vigorously as I could have or I would be in some sort of pain? Had I given him permission to do this by not fighting harder? Had I wanted this'? I wondered.

He silently walked me through the field, across the road and stopped when we reached the safety of homes and streetlights. He wiped down my jeans, which had very little dirt on them on the account of the ground being frozen.

'Be careful walking up that road, it's icy as shit and stick to the bits that are well lit' he delicately warned me before turning in the opposite direction and disappearing into the darkness.

As I walked home I felt lucky to be alive. I had this sense of relief that he hadn't killed me. He could have, it was so dark and there was no-one around, he surely would have gotten away with it if he wanted to. Yes, he had hurt me, but it could have been much worse. I didn't physically die that night, no, but I was about to learn just how much I wish he had killed me and how there was so much worse things someone could do to you than end your life.

As I walked towards the house, I didn't cry. I didn't feel I needed to. I held both arms out in front of me and just like I had done so many times before in PE, I swung them around in big circles. No pain. I bent both knees and lifted my legs out in front of and behind me. No pain. I swirled my head around, stretching my neck. No pain. With my toes pointing forward and my lower body still, I held my arms out straight at my sides and twisted to the left, then the right. No pain. I felt no bumps on my face or head, my stomach felt normal. I was fine. I would be okay. I was violently shaking, but was it from the cold or the attack? Maybe I were in shock. I had never been in shock before and didn't know what that felt like.

As I walked through the front door of my aunt and uncle's home, they asked where Diane was. 'You were right, I should have stayed home. I didn't feel great so Diane and Kaylee walked me to the roundabout before going back to Kaylee's' I lied.

'Did you fall? Are you okay'? A distant voice asked. I wasn't sure which one of them had said it but I nodded and told them I had slipped on black ice. My aunt hugged me and told me to have a shower to warm up. As I climbed into the shower I looked at my body for any signs of what just happened. I could find none. I had no cuts or bruises, no marks at all.

'Had it really happened? Did I have a fever and imagine it all? Surely if this had happened, there would be some evidence of it somewhere' I thought to myself. I dried and dressed in my pyjamas. As I walked into Diane's room, I noticed a hot water bottle laying on the bed and a mug of hot chocolate on the nightstand. I smiled to myself, crawled into bed, hugged the water bottle but was too exhausted to lift the mug of hot chocolate and I fell asleep. I was sharing Diane's double bed and didn't wake when she got home.

When I woke in the morning, I thought it had all been a terrifying dream, then I tried to move and realised the dream had been reality. Every muscle in my body had seized. As I attempted to lift my arms, they twitched in pain. I lifted the sleeves of my pyjamas to find huge purple welts had appeared overnight on my snow-white skin. I attempted to stand and felt the same pain in my legs but I dared look at them, looking at my arms had been enough. I was grotesque. I walked through the pain to the bathroom and nothing appeared broken. I was glad of this as I wouldn't have to explain to anyone what happened. As I looked at my face I saw a cut above my eye and was pleased to find very little bruising on my face and neck. 'Had the cut been there the night before? I hadn't noticed it' I wondered.

I stayed in bed all day. I was asked if I wanted to go home but I didn't want to leave that bed and face what had happened. Diane and I spent the day watching movies and eating junk food. My pyjamas had long sleeves and bottoms and covered my full body so I didn't notice all the marks that had appeared until I showered on Monday morning. By now I did have a bruise on my cheek but everyone was happy to believe this was from the fall on black ice and I was not about to correct them.   It was still winter which made it easy to cover the bruising until it disappeared.

Chapter 5

The second week after that fateful night I saw Alex sitting in his car in the school carpark as I left school. It was a busted-up silver car, there was rust on the bonnet and on the roof and the back passenger side door had a large dent in it. I froze. I hadn't seen him since that night.

The passenger door opened and a guy slowly got out. He was wearing a Reebok tracksuit; the jacket was mainly navy with a green stripe across the shoulders and a red triangle going from his right shoulder to his left hip. He had matching bottoms and plain white trainers that were covered in mud. He had been laughing as he exited the car but as his gaze fell on me, he looked almost repulsed.

'Get in the car', Alex's voice boomed from the driver's seat. 'I know where you live. Diane told us. We came all this way to pick you up, so you didn't have to walk home in the rain. Wasn't that nice of us? Get in'. I hadn't noticed the change in weather, and only then did I hear the pitter-patter of rain as it hit against the roof of his car.

He said he knew where I live. Was this true? Had Diane told him? I had no way of asking her. As I stood there contemplating my choices, I realised I didn't have any at all. I had been late out of class due to my first interrogation into the almost over-night change in my behaviour and attitude and there was no-one else around to run to for help. The door I excited from had been a fire door and closed behind me. I could have ran to reception but it was quite far and I was still stiff and in pain from Saturday night, they surely would have caught me. 'It'll be fine', I lied to myself before taking a few steps and getting into the car.

'Good girl' the friend whispered in my ear as he leaned across me, buckling my seat belt before standing back and laughing as he slamming the door closed.

'How was school'? Alex asked.

'Fine' I replied. 'What is he doing here'? I wondered to myself. 'Was he here to hurt me again? Maybe him bringing his friends was a scare tactic, or maybe he informed them what he had done a few nights prior and they were now here to get in on the action'. I told myself to calm down, closing my eyes and reminding myself I had made it through that night and would make it through whatever was about to come my way.

'Just fine? Is that all I get'? He smiled. Well, I had learned if you don't add the correct ingredients to your jam roll, it won't roll. Accounting was not something I wanted to do with my life even though I was good at it. The answers to Pythagoras's Theorem would never be found inside my brain and that McBeth could almost put me to sleep after listening, discussing, quoting, and acting it out for two straight hours.

'Just the usual school stuff; cooking, Maths, English' I responded trying to calm my quivering voice so he wouldn't know how scared I was.

'Look at me when I'm talking to you!' he shouted. I jumped and they all laughed together, his two friends in the backseat high-fiving each other.

'Ha-ha you tell her who's boss man' drifted forward as someone hit my chair from behind. I looked at Alex. He had a cigarette hanging from his lips, a scar across his left eyebrow that I hadn't noticed before, and what looked like a cut on his chin from shaving. His hands were on the wheel and as I studied them, they appeared so normal, yet I could have sworn they had been bigger.

He was wearing an Adidas tracksuit; it was navy, and the zipper was done all the way up to his neck. There was a tiny tear at his left elbow and he was wearing matching bottoms. He again smelled of Cool Waters aftershave, just as he had done three nights prior; it was so over-powering I could almost taste it.

As I sat there watching him, I realised I was no longer afraid. I wasn't panicking. I wasn't worried. I didn't care who saw me in the car, I felt nothing. I was numb and ready for whatever was about to happen to me. We drove around town for thirty-minutes, aimlessly going nowhere before Alex asked where I lived. Ha! He didn't know this! Was I surprised by his previous lie? No.

'Near the school' I replied, and he turned the car around.

'Tell me when to stop' I was instructed.

'At this bus stop is fine', I said. But he had not driven all this way to drop me off at a bus stop.

'I want to see where you live' he demanded. So, what did I do? I gave him step-by-step directions straight to my garden gate. Why did I do that? I told this monster where I lived. I had brought him to my home. If anything happened now, I only had myself to blame. How more stupid could I have been?

He leaned over, squeezed my right leg with his left hand and kissed me roughly on the cheek. 'Be a good girl', was the last words I heard as he unbuckled my seat belt and gestured for me to leave. I walked into the house, went upstairs, and headed straight to the bathroom. No-one was home and I was glad I didn't need to partake in meaningless small take. I spent the next twenty-minutes throwing up. As I sat on the cold bathroom floor my full body furiously shook, my legs were like jelly, my chest tightened and I was finding it difficult to breathe. I couldn't stand or see straight and all I could do was hold my head in my hands and wait for it to pass.

When it did, I sat staring at my shoes, still afraid my legs wouldn't hold me if I dared stand. They were black patent slip on shoes with a fake silver buckle. I can still close my eyes and remember them so clearly.

***

When I was around sixteen, I went to the cinema with a friend one night. I can't remember what we went to see but I do remember it being just the two of us sitting at the back row and halfway down was a father and daughter. That was it, just the four of us.

About twenty-minutes into the film, four people barged into the screening laughing loudly, pushing each other around and spilling popcorn everywhere. I turned around and there was Alex staring me in the face with a sinister look. He walked straight up to us, the others following behind as they sat down. I didn't remember seeing them outside and I was always hyper vigilant these days. Did they followed us and I hadn't noticed or was it sheer coincidence that they had found me there?

'Do you know them'? My friend asked. I shook my head no. 'They're quite sexy don't you think'? I looked at her with surprise. Did I think they were sexy? No, I didn't. Dangerous was a word more fitting for them.

After a few minutes, his two friends pulled out a packet or cigarettes. 'Want a draw'? They looked at my friend who smiled back.

'You can't go with them'! I pulled her arm as she started to stand. 'You don't even know them'! But she was already infatuated with one of them as they walked out together. She was the type of girl who craved attention, any attention from the opposite sex, and she would do just about anything to be noticed by older boys.

With them leaving, this allowed Alex and his friend to close in on me, sitting on either side. I was wearing an over-sized jumper and pulled the sleeves right down, holding tightly onto the cuffs so my hands were covered as I pulled my legs up to my chest. Alex didn't seem to notice, or maybe he did and just didn't care.

He leaned over and kissed my neck. His hands were exploring my full body as I sat there rigid. 'Shame we're at the pictures or I'd be all over you right now' he informed me.

'Lucky, I'm lucky we're at the cinema right now' I told myself. Our friends returned after 10-minutes and Alex removed his hand from my leg, his lips from my neck, stood up and helped my friend into her seat, kissing her hand as she took her seat. Everyone sat together, sharing popcorn and drinks while watching the rest of the movie. Everyone except me. I sat staring at the back of the empty chair in front of me, praying the movie would end so I could get my friend far away from them and return home to curl up in bed. At the end of the movie, we all got up and walked outside.

'How are you kids getting home'? One of his friends enquired.

'Getting the bus', my friend answered.

'Kids'? I laughed to myself. I stopped being a kid the night Alex held me down and ravaged my adolescence. 'Please don't say you'll give us a ride, I pleaded with them inside my head'. It had been an excruciating two hours and I was so ready for it to be over.

'Get home safe' replied Alex with a smile. They walked to the car park, we walked to the bus station, and it was over.

***

It wasn't always bad when I saw Alex; Whether it was him alone or he had his gang of cheerleaders with him, sometimes nothing bad happened at all. Occasionally, he would pick me up from school and take me for a burger, always to the same fast-food restaurant and he would never ask me to pay. We would sit at the same table in the back and he would talk at me as though we were friends. I haven't been back to any of those fast-food chains since those days. If it was a sunny day he would take me for ice cream, always a cone with raspberry sauce, this I never had a say in. We would sit in parks or on benches and again I would listen to him talking but never really taking anything in. I rarely eat ice cream anymore.

A few times he would take me shopping with him, usually for new trainers. He had a thing about trainers. I mean, his car would have been rejected by the scrap yard, his hair always looked like it needed to be washed and cut, most of his clothes had cigarettes burns or were worn but if his trainers got the tiniest bit of mud on them, he went straight out and bought new ones without attempting to first clean them up.

This one day, I had been waiting at the bus stop as I was going ice skating and meeting my friends there, when his car pulled up. 'I need knew gutties, get in', I was ordered. And I did. We went shopping for new trainers and were in a few different stores as he tried on trainer after trainer. He finally settled in one store and had three pairs that he liked when the shop assistant asked him which ones he wanted to buy. 'Better ask my girlfriend' he laughed and pointed at me.

'Ask his girlfriend'? Was he really that neurotic that he thought I was his girlfriend for the day? Is this how he saw me or was it meant as a joke? Had I done something, lead him on in some way for him to think this? Was this full thing my fault? Had I lead him on that first night we met, or the second night when I let him walk with me without fighting back? I could never think of him as my boyfriend. As panic struck in, he laughed and pointed to a pair of white Reebok trainers.

'I think she liked those ones better'. They were £35 and he made me pay for every penny in the car on the way home as he pulled over at two different bus stops. The first one was only a few minutes from the store we had just left. At this one, he pulled my head back by my hair and kissed my neck. His kisses were wet, and his tongue was rough, but I knew better by now than to pull away or complain. His right hand was under my t-shirt, and he was pulling at the front of my bra. 'Fuck this shit' he deafeningly cried out and punched the steering wheel as a bus honked behind him to move his car.

He angrily drove for ten-minutes before coming to a stop at the second bus stop where he had his right hand firmly clasped on my neck, his thumb pushing strong against my vocal cords. He fiercely pulled my right hand and placed it between his legs, his left hand now between mine. I could feel how excited he was and knew how this went. 'Just get him off quickly with your hand and maybe he won't have time to force your head down there too' I reasoned with myself.

'What would your parents say if they saw you now'? He whispered in my ear. 'What would they say'? I quietly wondered to myself. 'Would they say it was my own fault? Would they ask why I let it go on for so long? Would they even care'?

Chapter 6

As I grew up, I had different jobs and moved a lot. The most I moved was six times in five years. Each time I moved home, I would eventually receive a bunch of flowers. These would be left on my doorstep, hand-delivered, or sent from a local florist.

If I changed jobs, he would always find me. Flowers would be sent there too. Every year on my birthday I received flowers; They were always the same, some pink bouquet with a card that read 'Happy Birthday Princess'. The bouquets were always beautiful, and I did like flowers. However, each one I got went directly into the bin. I couldn't have a part of him in my home

In my mid-twenties, I was in college and working part-time in a pizza place. I worked in the kitchen and was never on the main floor. My manager walked in during the lunch shift and told me that my cousins were in the restaurant. It was a quiet, mid-week afternoon, so I washed my hands, took off my apron and walked onto the floor.

There he was; him and two others. One of them was wearing a big plastic 'Happy Birthday' badge attached to his green polo shirt front. 'It's Sinky's birthday', I was told. 'You said come in for birthday pizza, remember'? He told me. I don't remember; it hadn't been mentioned to me. They wanted a large 'special birthday' pizza with all the toppings. I walked back into the kitchen and got to making this. I evenly spread out the tomato base, carefully placed all the toppings just as I had been trained to do and covered it all in our three-grated cheese mix. I put the pizza, garlic bread slices, and two different kinds of chicken wings into the oven. 'I'll give him extra; hopefully, it'll put him in a good mood, and he'll leave as soon as they're done', I prayed to myself. They ate everything; thanked my boss for the service and left. I was left with the bill.

A few years later, I started a new part-time job in my local pub and was really enjoying it. One night, I was working at the bar, which was my favourite bar to work in. It had two pool tables and access to the beer garden. Our pool team played that night, and the bar was busier than usual.

I stepped away for a few minutes to get a fresh bottle of vodka as we were going through it quicker than normal; as I stepped back onto the bar; my back was to everyone while changing the bottle over.

'Alright, Lux'? People always used nicknames with me; very rarely these days did anyone call me Lux, except him; he always used my name. My whole body shuddered. My teeth were chattering, and my hands trembled so much I couldn't screw the lid back on the bottle.

I slowly turned around, waiting with bated breath to see what fate had in store for me on this night. 'Make it a double for my boys,' he sneered at me. They sat at the booth on the left-hand side of the bar and waited for their drinks.

'Who's those drinks for'? The person in charge asked me.

'The guys in the corner', I said without looking at the table.

'Did they pay'? She inquired.

'I'll pay, they're friends', I quietly lied. She carried the drinks over, and a wave of relief washed over me. Friends? Is this my lie now?

They stayed until closing, keeping quiet to themselves in a bar full of laughter and cheering. I could feel his stare trying to pierce my soul as I carried on with my work. When the last order bell rang, I was told they would take their drinks in the beer garden.

I attended to the rest of the bar's people, poured his drinks, and carried them outside. 'What have I told you about getting a new job'? He reminded me. 'I'll find you anywhere you go. You can't hide from me. We'll give you a lift home', I was swiftly told. And they did. They drove me home and watched from the car as I unlocked my front door, stepped inside then they drove off. I was exhausted.

We often had different acts booked at the weekend in the pub. I remember this one weekend; we had all been rota'd on as there was a live gig, and we had sold all the tickets. A few days before the event, I got a call saying the band had cancelled due to personal reasons, so I wouldn't be needed that night.

I liked the people I worked with; we all got along and had a lot of fun together. A few minutes later, one of them called me, 'We're meeting in the pub at 6 pm Friday, we'll grab food, then we're all going bowling', I was told.

I'll be there', I said excitedly.

I headed straight to the bar after my full-time job and was there at 5.30 pm. 'Pick your poison; you lot will need drinks to win anything', my manager laughed.

'Vodka, double', I smiled in agreement. My colleagues started arriving, and by 6.30 pm, we had left the pub and were standing in our lane, arguing about whose name went on the board first and whether we wanted bumpers or not.

We laughed so hard that night. I have no idea who won; I don't remember if we finished playing the second game or not before we headed into the bar, filled with Dutch courage, and signed each other up for karaoke.

It was my turn for drinks, so up to the bar I walked, taking with me our empty glasses, always the barmaid. I handed over the list of our drinks (we were going through their cocktail and shots list, a different one each round) when someone came up behind me, put their hands over my eyes, and told me to open my mouth. I laughed and said I wasn't tasting anything that didn't come from the bar staff.

'I've got something for you to taste. Get on your knees;' those words were a rapidly sobering experience.

I stood, my feet frozen on the sticky bar floor. I could hear my heart pounding in my ears over the music as my hands began to sweat. My brain became overloaded with fear, and a panic attack set in. I couldn't think; my thoughts scattered. He brought one hand down and around the front of my throat while the other pulled my hair back and he kissed my neck.

The bartender set the drinks in front of her and looked at me worryingly. I saw her glance at my friends, and before I could think, one of them grabbed Alex and pushed him hard to the floor. He jumped up. They were face to face; Alex's eyebrows were lowered and pulled close together, his lips tightened, and his jaw tense.

'She's my girlfriend, mate', he spat.

'Funny coz she's my sister, and she didn't mention anything about seeing a wasted stinking relic like you', my friend defended me. The bar staff threw him out, and a few minutes later, my phone started lighting up with missed calls and texts. I put it in my pocket and tried to pretend everything was fine.

The following Monday, I left work and walked through the carpark of the building next door. It was 7.30 pm, and the carpark was deserted. I turned the corner to access the road, and he was there. He was standing outside his beaten-up rusted red car. All his new cars looked old.

He was alone, which was unusual for him. He walked towards me, without saying a word and punched me square in the face. I hit the floor as he threw his second punch, then his third. A warm wet feeling escaped down my mouth; a sharp stinging left on the bridge of my nose. I bit my tongue and could taste the blood pooling in my mouth. This was not the first time he gifted me with a black eye.

Even though all I wanted to do was get home, I got off the bus a few stops early as I felt people's eyes on me, even though this meant a long walk and a rather large bridge to cross. It was a clear night, and as I reached the centre of the bridge, I stopped and looked around me at the sea of lights in the distance from people's homes. I looked down; it was a high height, and there were plenty of cars passing underneath; all I had to do was jump, and it would be over. I had been fighting extremely hard for so long, and I knew I couldn't handle much more. Would death be my only freedom from this nightmare?

***

In my mid twenty's, I started working for an energy company. I had zero faith that I would even last the six-week training programme, but as it worked out, I loved my job! There were so many people, teams, coaches, managers, and different jobs, and I wanted to know everything I could about them. And through my eight years of working there, I eventually did.

My days were never boring. They were fast-paced, exciting, challenging, sometimes soul-crushing, and was mostly me tied to a desk working on an investigation, trying to calm down a highly irate customer over the phone who had made an agent cry, dealing with ombudsman complaints and lawyer's letters, making up training programmes and being there for everyone all at the same time while living on coffee, energy drinks and cigarettes. I would stop smoking for months; then I would see Alex, and boom, I would start again.

I continued to get regular visits from Alex and his 'best boys' as he was now calling them. Never all at the same time. In total, including Alex, there were six of them.

The building where I worked was a 20-minute walk from the closest bus stop. For a period, my regular shifts were 11.am –7.15 pm Monday to Friday. When I left work at night, it was deserted. Maybe three cars were in the carpark, and one was the works pool car. I could either take the stairs from our carpark to the road, which had no lighting, and was surrounded on both sides with trees and bushes or I could walk through the carpark of the empty building next to us and, from here, the road was quite better with a mini roundabout, a small row of shops and a huge wide road.

So many nights I would leave work, there he would be, standing or leaning against his car. Sometimes alone, or with friends. Sometimes he would smile and stare as I walked past; other times, he would tell me to get into the car, which I would do, which I would always do without fighting back. I had learned over the years it was better to give into his demands; it was better to just give up.

Occasionally, he would leave the car with whoever happened to be with him that day, and he would walk me to the bus stop. During these times, he would stand on my right side, blocking me from the few passing cars. The road was always quiet at that time of the night as the business's around us closed early. He would put his left arm over my shoulders like you would see when someone held another person in a chock hold, and he would grab my neck with his left hand.

Then he would kiss me. He kissed my neck, my cheek, and my lips.

If he didn't feel I was 'into it' enough, he would push me to my knees and pull my hair causing my head to snap back. 'You're not a fucking princess', he would remind me, then pull me back up by my hair, and we would continue walking. Or he would knock me to my knees, kick me in the stomach, press his head hard against mine, then pull me up, and we would continue walking. I never once thought of myself as a princess, and he surely never made me feel like one.

He would either walk me to the bus stop, wait for 30 to 40 minutes for the bus to arrive, and then call his friends, who would drive his car down and pick him up. Or he would get on the bus with me, stay for a few stops, and then call for them to come pick him up.

During these agonising times, he would talk about anything and nothing. What he had done that day or week, what he was having for dinner; he was always hungry and looking for food. He would talk about music. 'Have you heard so and so's new song/album? It was sound'! What really went through his head during these times? Did he think we were friends?

One night, it must have been dead of winter because I remember it was so dark outside, almost black, and it was freezing cold. I was pulling on my black leather gloves and didn't see his car right away as it was parked further up the road than it usually was. I heard someone yell out; I thought they were in trouble, so I spun around. I knew instantly the person in trouble was about to be me.

He half walked; half stumbled. His eyes were huge, glaring at me, and he was spitting as he yelled at me. When he got close enough, I smelled the alcohol on his breath. I had seen him drunk before, but never like this. His face was red, he had this hostile glare, his lip was curled, and his jaw clenched tight. He swung at my head and missed.

'Wow, he can miss,' I thought to myself, never having witnessed that before. This enraged him. He lunged at me, trying to grab my shoulders, but he lost his footing. It may have been the ice, or plausibly his drunken stake, but we fell backwards, with me on my back and him on top of me. Just like that night when this all started. His friends were instantly at him, trying to pull him off me as he continued to swing at my body with closed fists.

'*YOU RUINED MY LIFE, YOU MOTHER-FUCKING BITCH! I FUCKING HATE YOU! YOU FUCKING SLUT! FUCKING BITCH! GET UP AND FIGHT BACK YOU FUCKING IDIOT! I'LL KILL YOU! YOU'RE FUCKING DEAD! YOU'VE RUINUED MY LIFE! ARE YOU LISTENING TO ME?! BITCH YOU'RE DEAD! YOU ARE DEAD! I WILL KILL YOU ONE DAY! THAT'S A FUCKING PROMISE! DON'T YOU KNOW WHO I AM?*' He screamed at me.

His two friends had managed to get him to his feet, one on either side, holding him up as he kicked me repeatedly in the stomach. Each kick exhaled all the air from my lungs, my shoulders curling forward. I gasped for breath.

As I lay on the cold ground, my eyes closed, in the foetal position, I heard the slamming of doors and felt the air hit my back as the car sped past me. His words circled my head. 'I hate you. You've ruined my life'. Funny, wasn't that how I was supposed to feel about him? Why did he hate me much? What had I ever done to him? I lay there at the side of the road, wanting to close my eyes and fall asleep, feeling incredibly sick and broken as I let out a torturous scream.

I brought up blood for the next three days. I never told anyone. I didn't see a doctor. That thought never crossed my mind. I called work the next day, got emergency annual leave, and I stayed home.

It was easy to hide. To hide myself, to hide my cuts and bruises. I rarely saw my family because I worked so much. We didn't have a uniform at work, and I would always wear a long-sleeved black cardigan over my shirt in the pub, even when I didn't have anything to hide. You can hide pretty much anything with a good concealer and good foundation. Wearing glasses instead of contact lenses hid bruising around the eye, and painkillers, lots of painkillers, allowed me to walk straight.

None of his friends ever did anything to me other than grab at me, hit me around the head a few times, and spit on me once. I was sitting in the passenger seat with Alex driving beside me one sunny day. One of his friends, his name was

Johnny, was pulling at my hair, then leaned forward past the headrest and kissed me hard on my right cheek.

Alex became insanely angry. He slammed on the brakes, got out of the car, pulled Johnny out by the sleeve of his jacket, punched him hard in the head, threw him to the ground then kicked him a few times. I dared turn around. I sat staring forward but could see enough from the corner of my eye to know what was going on. He leaned over him. 'Nobody touches her but me, you fucking dick'! Then he got in the car and drove away, leaving him lying there on the ground. I was terrified to speak.

✳✳✳

Infrequently, my dad would drive around and visit his close family. I always went with him. I was a big family person and loved seeing everyone as much as I could. On this particular day, we had done all the rounds and were returning home when my dad suddenly headed for Diane's house.

I was happy about this as I hadn't seen her in a few weeks because it was during our exams and she was studying pretty hard. We parked outside the house and could hear voices coming from the backyard. We made our way to the voices and found my uncle and Diane dismantling an old, busted hut so they could build a new bigger one. I laughed as soon as I saw Diane, as she was not the type of girl to get her hands dirty.

'Need a hand'? My dad asked.

'That would be great,' my uncle replied, wiping sweat from his brow with his arm.

'More helpers! This thing will be built in no time at all,' came my aunt's voice from the open kitchen window.

'Sure, will be,' I heard from behind me. I knew that voice. It couldn't be. It wasn't. I stood still as Alex walked in front of me towards my uncle with a bottle of water, stopping half-way and winking at me. Apparently, Alex was driving past, saw my uncle struggling with the old shed and stopped to help. Wasn't he just great? No. He could fool a lot of people, but he could never fool me.

I sat on the step and watched the four of them working. Before long, the men had their tops off as the sun continued to beat down. I sat there analysing Alex's body. I hadn't realised until now that I had never seen it before. I had felt it, but I had never seen it. Only now did I see his sculpted muscles, toned abs, and tanned skin. He had trained as a boxer for a few years prior but had to stop due to an injury, but he continued working out. If I didn't know the person under the skin, I would have thought he looked pretty handsome.

I continued to stare as they continued to work. Normally, I would be right in there getting dirty and helping break things up, carrying them into the van to be disposed of, and keeping everyone's energy levels up by being silly, but I thought it best to sit this one out. I remained on the step, and when asked, I said I wasn't feeling great.

Over the years, Alex attended Diane's 18th and 21st birthday parties. He had been there at her graduation party and even attended a family wedding on her dad's side as

Diane's plus-one. Everyone who met him thought he was marvellous. And now, so did my dad. I sat there laughing, thinking to myself what would happen if I opened my mouth and told my dad, my uncle, the guy they were laughing with, sharing stories with, bonding with, was the same guy who had stolen my virginity at fourteen and had become a staple of torture in my life ever since. I wondered if he would tell them he knew me, saying something ridiculous like we had hung out a few times, or he had picked me up and given me a ride somewhere. I quietly pleaded with him not to say anything.

Then something peculiar started to happen. I started to doubt myself. I sat there questioning whether or not he was a nice guy. Had I just not seen it? Diane liked him; her friends liked him, her parents liked him, and now my dad. Was I the crazy one? Was I not seeing something they all did? Yes, that night, he had been a monster but was there more to him? Had he done what he did that night because he was angry or drunk? Had someone hurt him? I never asked him why; maybe I should have.

Then I started to remember everything he had done to me. Everything he had ever said. All the ways he had chipped away at my soul until I was an empty shell, and I realised I was the only one who knew the real Alex.

He had even encouraged his friend one night to kill me. We were sitting in his car, driving somewhere, and Alex was yelling at me for something. His friend called out from the back seat, reminding him he was a mechanic and all Alex had to do was give him the nod, and he would mess with the car brakes. Alex had laughed and told him he liked his plan and would one day take him up on his offer. I have tried to learn how to drive over the years but the thought of someone playing with the brakes on my car to kill me has never left my head. How could I ever put someone else in danger? Someone who could be in the car with me or another driver that I may hit and kill as I lost control. I would never forgive myself if anyone else got hurt because of me.

Chapter Seven

I worked with the energy company for 8 years. One afternoon, I was sitting at my desk working on an investigation and I was just having a bad day. I was tired; it was hot, the make-up covering my latest black eye was beginning to run down my face and all I wanted was to go home, have a cold shower, drink a pint of ice water, and not have to adult that day. But I had work to do, a meeting to head and deadlines to meet.

I worked on the investigation for about half an hour and knew I was getting nowhere fast. I looked around for a coach but they were either on a break or on a call, so I apprehensively approached my manager for help. Now, I had never done so before because I could always, eventually, work out any problem on my own but here I was, standing at her desk, asking for her help. My manager Lucy was sitting at her desk. She was dressed in black trousers, a grey t-shirt, her brown shoulder length hair was blowing as a fan attached to her desk spun around on high power. I liked Lucy, she was funny, could relate to all of us and was easy to talk to.

'Lucy, I need your help, I can't work out this account. I'm too hot and too tired to think, do you have a minute to look over it with me'? I asked.

Lucy looked at me for a few seconds without saying a word. I thought maybe I should have waited on a coach instead; they had more experience on working with accounts after all. Yes, lucy was a manager but I wasn't sure how much knowledge she had about the detailed workings of an investigation. 'I'll give it a go' she smiled at me.

Lucy stood up, took my book with my workings in it and asked me to follow her. I thought this was strange as people usually used their own computers to look at things but maybe she didn't have access to the systems I used on her computer and didn't want to sit at my desk in front of our team. We walked into this tiny office; it had a desk against one wall with a chair at either side, three walls were painted green and the wall facing into the room had two floor length windows covered by old cream horizontal blinds that hadn't seen a duster or a cloth in a while. Lucy closed the blinds on the windows but left the blind covering the square window at the top of the door open. 'Sit down' she gently told me and pointed to the empty chair in front of the window.

'Lux this isn't about the account. I can see your black eye. You can talk to me' she started.

'Here we go again, I thought'.

'Lucy I just need help with this account, I can't work it out. Everything I'm trying adds up and I can't find what caused the problem. If you can't help me, I can go find a coach who can'.

I started to stand and saw another manager, Margaret standing outside looking through the window in the door. Lucy jumped up, looked at Margaret, closed the blinds and again told me to sit down but by this point I was over the account and had a lot more work I could be doing rather than sitting in that jail like office.

'Look, I'm just tired, it's hot and I've been here since 7.am. Can you please either look at the account or let me get on with something else? I have a meeting in an hour', I pleaded with her. She picked up my book and we started going through my workings. Less than ten-minutes later, Margaret came barging into the office.

'I need you both to follow me' she declared. I thought something had happened on the floor, so I jumped up and followed her. She walked off the floor, pushed G on the lift panel and we got inside. When we got to the ground floor, I asked what was going on.

'Follow me' Margaret stated, giving no further explanation. We turned left, through a set of fire doors and walked into the first aid room.

The room was square, had a few cupboards on one wall, windows on two others and six scattered chairs. Lucy closed all the blinds before her and Margaret pulled two chairs together and sat down in front of the only door. I suddenly had a sinking feeling this was not about any account as my eyes darted around the room looking for another way out.

'Lux, please sit down' Lucy asked. I was trapped, the only way out was blocked by the both of them and I could feel the tension building.

'Relax' I told myself. 'You've talked yourself out of worse situations than this and you'll do the same thing now. Just listen and nod, say anything you need to in order to convince them everything is over and that you're fine. Don't forget to smile' I reminded myself. As they were sitting closest to the door, I choose a seat at the opposite end of the room and sat down.

Lucy and Margaret glanced at each other for a few seconds as though having a private conversation together in their minds then Margaret spoke. 'Don't panic' she started. Always a good way to start a conversation I half laughed to myself. 'But I've called the police and they're on their way to talk with us'.

I felt the air escape my lungs and was unable to speak for a few minutes. 'And why did you do that'? I enquired.

'Because this is the last time I watch you come in here with another bruise or cut or black eye and if you're not going to tell us what's going on then you'll speak to the police' she informed me.

I stood up and walked towards the door. 'Lux please, sit down. I promise it's going to be okay' pleased Lucy. 'I promise you are safe here; we'll take this at your pace, you're the one in charge. If you want us to stay with you or if you want us to leave, just say'. I took another step towards the door.

Lucy continued 'Do you remember last week when you changed shifts and I thought you were late to work? I sat at my desk for half an hour worried sick that something had happened to you, that you had been killed before scheduling finally got back to me about the shift change. I feel awful because I can see something is going on and I haven't done anything about it. I will not have you die on me Lux. I will not live with that on my conscious'.

I stood there, frozen to the spot. 'She thought I were dead? That must have been awful for her. I can't do this to anyone. I can't have anyone be that worried about me' I thought to myself. I slowly sat down, took a few deep breaths, rubbed my hands together and tried to think how I could escape this one. I had always thought if I acted like everything was fine then no-one would notice anything was wrong. But this had clearly not been the case.

They were both talking to me. I could see their lips moving and I could hear something, but it was muffled like my head was being held under water. Lucy walked up to me 'It'll be alright' she said as she hugged me. 'We're right here with you and won't leave unless you want us to' she went on.

'If you're scared, or you need a minute or you need to take a break just look at me and I'll stop it. I'll take you outside for some air then we can come back in'. My hand's had starting to shake, my breathing quickened. Lucy kneeled in front of me, taking my hands in hers. 'Shh, it's okay, just breath. I've got you; I promise it will all be okay'.

We sat there in silence until the police arrived twenty-minutes later. The man was about my dad's age, he had black hair that was greying around his ears and a slight beard. The female with him looked younger than me. She had red hair pulled back, freckles across her nose and cheeks and her eyes were soft as she smiled at me.

'There's a lot of people in this room eh'? The male officer declared. 'Does everyone have to be here'? He questioned.

'Please don't leave' I finally said looking at Lucy and Margaret. I was so angry at them for doing this, for betraying me like this, but I was scared and didn't want to be alone.

'We're not going anywhere' Lucy said as she squeezed my hand and pulled a chair closer to me. 'You're doing the right thing talking with the police'.

'Then why does it feel so wrong'? I asked, tears filling up my eyes.

'So, what's going on here'? The male officer asked as he took a seat. I couldn't speak. It was as though the signals between my mouth and brain had been severed and I had forgotten how to.

'We'll tell them what we've seen' declared Margaret nodding at me for approval. I sat there in silence as I listened to them both telling the officers about how they've seen me with several black eyes. How I had a broken wrist two months before. How I always looked like I were in pain and took painkillers 'like they were skittles'. They went on to say how I had lost weight, that I didn't eat, and lived on coffee and ProPlus. I sat there a little confused, I had always thought I were doing a good job at covering everything up but apparently not. I should have done a better job! How could I have been so careless?!

The officers started asking me questions. 'Do you agree with what they are telling us? Is there someone hurting you?

Do you need help? Are you in danger today? Can you tell us what happened to your eye'? They were taking turns speaking but they both had the same look on their faces. Their eyebrows were angled down, their mouth and lips drawn in tightly, like they were feeling sorry for whatever was happening to me.

I sat there thinking 'I don't need those pitiful expressions, your soft words, and the deafening silence between your questions. I am not a child. I am not going to break; you have no idea how much I have gone through and you both sitting in front of me is not going to break me. I've come too far for this'. But I stayed silent.

I suddenly thought about the time. What if Alex had been outside and saw them come in? He surely would know they were here to see me! He told me time and time again he would kill me if I ever opened my mouth. I realised if I wanted this to be over, and I did as quickly as possible, then I would have to give them something. I had to get rid of them before it was too late.

I told them I had been getting hassle from someone but that I had dealt with it and it was over now. I promised Lucy and Margaret I would never come into work again looking like the way I did now. They pressed for more information, but I wouldn't say anything else.

They informed me as a concern had been raised that they needed me to come down to the police station and close it off. At the time I was living with my gran who was sick and I had to go straight home. Lucy told them she would bring me down the following day and they left.

'I need a cigarette' I said out loud.

'I didn't know you smoked' they replied in unison. 'Sometimes we need a way of killing ourselves in order to stay alive' I silently replied.

Lucy drove me to the police station the next afternoon. We sat in this small office to the right of the reception desk and the male officer from the day before asked me if I wanted to give any more information or press charges. I said no.

'People who pop in and out of your life sporadically and hurt you usually have a criminal record. One of the reasons you don't see them for periods of time is because they are usually in jail for 28 days at a time. I can't force you to talk or press charges. The concern will be closed off today but please do not hesitate to contact us if you change your mind or need help in the future' he told me. 'You too' he looked at Lucy before telling me I was lucky to have people in my life who cared that much for me. I did feel lucky, but not for the reason he was stating. I felt lucky Alex hadn't been waiting for me when I finished work the night before and I was lucky he wasn't sitting in the car park as I left with Lucy that morning.

Chapter Eight

In 2009 Alex moved over 300 miles to live with an aunt. She was older, lived alone as her husband passed years before from a heart attack and her own children had all grown and moved on. I never asked if this were the reason for his move.

He got a job working on a building site and was apparently doing really well. I found this out through Diane about six weeks after he left and at first I honestly wasn't sure how to feel about it. I didn't really believe he was so far away. He had always been so close, a huge part of my life for the last nine years and now he was in another country. I didn't instantly jump for joy at this news as he still felt so close.

I immediately wondered if he would find someone else to torture. This thought consumed me, thinking of him finding another soul to crush would surely be my fault. I should have had the courage to speak up, to tell someone what was going on, I couldn't live with anyone else being hurt because of my weakness. I had to tell someone, now, but who? Where would I start? Did it even matter at this point? It was no longer about me. Someone else could be in danger and I had to do everything I could to save them before their life mirrored mine.

I was at work on a Friday night when I got the phone call about his relocation and most people had already gone home. I still had an hour before I finished and I decided in that time I would go directly to Lucy first thing Monday morning, tell her the truth, and ask her to come with me to the police station.

On Monday morning I arrived at work early. I got myself a coffee from the machine and took a seat in the corner of the canteen. It was empty, not even the chef had arrived yet but today was the day where I had to put myself, my thoughts, my feelings, my fears aside and think of his next victim. I sat there until 7:30am then slowly got up and made my way upstairs to my desk.

Lucy was rarely in the office before 10am so I had time to think about what I would say. I knew when I told her the truth, she would automatically focus on me so I had to swiftly get her attention focused on what he could do to someone else. I had to make her understand what kind of monster he was and if that meant spilling all my deepest darkest secrets to her, then that was exactly what I was ready to do.

I took my seat and switched on my computer. I was the first member of my team to arrive so I stood up and turned on everyone else's computer. This was something we did for each other to make it quicker logging in each morning. It only took me a few minutes and when I returned to my desk I noticed a missed call from Diane. She never called me this early.

I picked up my phone, left the floor and made my way to the stairwell to call her back. She was sobbing down the phone and I couldn't understand a word she was saying. When she finally calmed down, I couldn't believe it. I walked down the stairs, making my way to the smoking area outside and stood there in shock. When I returned to my desk, I spent the day staring at my screen, clicking a few keys, and aimlessly moving my mouse around so it looked like I were doing some work.

Alex had gone to the pub on Friday after work and had some drinks. He obviously had more than he thought because when he left he got behind the wheel of his car to drive home. He was in the car alone and it appeared he had lost control, come off the road, down an embankment and stopped when he crashed into a wooden fence. He was in a coma and the doctors said there was nothing they could do for him. His mum and brother were on their way down. Three days later, Diane called back to inform me his mum had made the decision to turn his life support off. He was gone.

He was gone? Dead? He couldn't be dead. He was invincible. Untouchable. Nothing bad could happen to him. She had to be mistaken. This didn't feel real. How had they confirmed it were him? Diane told me he suffered severe injuries to his face, maybe it were someone else who had driven his car? Police and doctors had made mistakes before, this surely was one of those times. A car crash couldn't end his life. Not Alex.

His mum wanted his body brought back home and that took some time to arrange. Diane spent a lot of time with his family over the next few days; cooking them meals, buying in shopping, helping them with funeral arrangements, being the go-between for everyone. She was a kind person and had really liked Alex. I often worried about her being around him, but he seemed to treat her more like a kid sister.

Diane, along with her friends, my aunt and uncle were going to the funeral and Diane asked me if I would go with her. This came as a complete shock to me.

'I know you didn't like him and only seen him a few times, but he always talked about you. I think he had a crush on you. He would ask me how you were, where you were working, if you were seeing anyone. I think he would like it if you came along. Please, I need you there"

I did not want to go. Funerals were a time and place for loved ones to say their final goodbyes. They were filled with sadness while also reminiscing and celebrating the life of their lost loved one. Diane told me some of his friends had written poems and his step-sister was going to sing a song during the service that reminded her of Alex.

I was hesitant to answer before having the opportunity to seriously think about it. If I went, I would feel like an imposter, sitting there amongst everyone who knew him, who would be missing him. I wasn't even sure how I felt about it. Was I happy he was gone? Would I get my life back? Was I sad a young life had been lost? Yes I felt sadness, I could see how much Diane was hurting and that hurt me. It didn't matter who he was to me, to her he was her friend. His family had lost a son, a brother, an uncle. It was sad. A funeral, after all, was supposed to be a celebration of someone's life and I didn't have anything to celebrate about Alex. 'I'll have to think about it' I told Diane.

As the days passed, it was all I could think about. It didn't feel real. Was he really gone? Would I truly never see him again? Was it really over? The more I thought about it, the more I realised I needed to go. I needed to know for sure. I needed to see for myself that he was gone. I needed closure. I called Diane and told her I would come along.

On the days leading up to the funeral, I felt awful. I couldn't sleep. My whole body ached and I was sick for days on end. On the day of the funeral, I got up early, showered, dressed, and made myself some toast. I sat there staring at the plate, unable to eat anything. I left my house and met up with Diane and her parents.

'Are you okay'? My uncle asked. 'You look awful'.

'I think I've picked up a bug' I replied. Diane hadn't noticed how I looked but I noticed her. Her eyes were red and swollen, she had been crying. I hugged her. He may be the person consuming my nightmares, but he had always been there for her.

As we neared the church I saw a sea of people in black. It was easy to recognise his friends as they held scarves and memorabilia from his favourite football team. As I watched his friends, the hearse drove directly in front of us. I saw the coffin in the back and his name spelled out in green and white flowers along one side. The coffin was mahogany and I caught a glimpse of the golden plaque on top which I assumed had his name carved into it. As the hearse turned the corner to the church, I saw the words 'son' and brother' spelled out in green and white flowers on the other side. He had been loved.

The next thing I remember was Diane and my uncle picking me up from the ground. Had I fainted or had my legs given way? A few of Diane's friends came over and asked if I were okay. I told them I was fine and had a bug. They all accepted this and my uncle told me he thought it best if I went to my grans house and lay down. My gran lived very close and I agreed.

As they walked towards the church, I stood for a few minutes watching the sea of people whose lives had been forever changed by his loss. Some were softly crying; others were hugging one another. I stood wondering if I were the only one there who were glad he was gone. I wasn't glad he were dead, but I was glad he was no longer part of my life.

I had never met his mum or brother but I immediately picked them out of the crowd. His brother was standing tall, his arms wrapped tightly around his grieving mother whose tears flowed down her cheeks. His brother looked very much like him and it scared me for a second.

I stood there in silence, taking in all the people who had loved him, who would miss him and I thought to myself how could one person touch so many lives in a positive way and yet ruin mine? He was a saint and a sinner. I don't believe in God or the Devil but I found myself wondering, if they did both exist, would Alex end up in Heaven or Hell?

As I stood looking at the hearse, I knew this was all the closure I needed. He was gone. It was real. I was free. I watched everyone slowly head inside. I saw his coffin being removed and carefully lifted by six men all in black suits. I watched as they made their way into the church, the music from the organ blaring out the open doors and I sighed. I felt as though his life ending would mean mine could finally begin again.

I walked to my grans house, changed into my pyjamas, and crawled into the spare bed, just as I had done so many times as a child. She brought me a bowl of home-made soup with a glass of milk; sat on the bottom of the bed chatting about her favourite TV show, her friends and what she needed at the supermarket. When I was done eating, she kissed me on my forehead, lifted the empty bowl and glass and softly closed the door. I stayed in that bed for two days, not having the will or the strength to move.

For a few months, everything was calm. I still lived my life on high alert. I was vigilant about my surroundings. I continued to pick out the exits everywhere I went. I tried not to go out on my own. For the first time in months, everything appeared calm. Was it finally over? Could I get my life back? What would a life without Alex look like? Could I finally walk outside and not be scared, not spend time looking over my shoulder? Did I still have to note the exits as soon as I walked into somewhere new? Could I go out with friends, relax, and finally enjoy myself? Maybe I could have a boyfriend and really try this time. What would that be like? Was this it?

I didn't have to wait long in having my questions answered as his friends casually slipped right in and took over where Alex had left. Even though they had been present for a lot of the times I saw or was with Alex, they were never as rough as him. The thought and hope of a normal life had been nice while it lasted though. I should have known better. This isn't how my life usually went.

Chapter Nine

I finished my shift at the call centre one Friday night and rushed home to change into my pub uniform. I didn't have time to run to the bank during my lunchbreak so I now had to walk to the nearest shop to use their cash machine so I could call a taxi to work. I left the house and hurriedly made my way along the road.

I had to pass through a set of garages with old, rusted doors. There were 15 on each side and as I walked I realised darkness was beginning to set in quicker these days. I was not fully paying attention to where I was going because I was already running late. I had my black Radley handbag on across my body and was looking in it for my phone to call work and inform them I would be a few minutes late when I felt a force pull me backwards and I fell to the ground. Then came the blows, from all directions. They were hard and fast.

I held my hands up to protect my face which left my body unprotected so I moved my hands to my stomach which left my face unprotected. I tried to open my eyes but I couldn't. I tried to stand but was repeatedly pushed back to the ground. I eventually gave up and lay there, taking everything they gave and waited for it to be over.

Before they stopped, I heard shouting and the sound of people running. When I finally opened my eyes, I saw four men fighting. Two were Alex's friends and two were men I didn't recognise. 'Had the four of them being attacking me and suddenly turned on each other'? I wondered.

As it turned out, the two men I didn't recognise happened to be walking past, saw what was happening and came to help me. The fighting had stopped and the two men were shouting at his friends to leave me alone. They ran to a parked car I remembered walking past and sped off as the other two men ran over to help me up. 'What's your name? Do you know where you are? Stay still, we'll get you an ambulance'.

'No' I shouted. 'I'm fine, I'm late for work. Thank you so much for helping me'. They said I should call the police and go to hospital to be checked over but as they realised I was not going to do either of these, one of them wrote down both their names and contact details on a napkin he pulled from his pocket and handed it to me.

'Call us if you change your mind and need witnesses' he said. They again asked if I were sure I didn't want to call the police or an ambulance but I thanked them, walked towards the cash machine where they stood guard, got into a waiting taxi, and headed to work.

The drive was only a few minutes. When I got there, I hung up my bag, put on my black cardigan and walked onto the function bar to start opening it up. The girl I was working with was already on the bar unlocking the shutters.

'Oh my god Lux what happened to you? Are you okay'?

'I'm fine' I told her as I pulled the fruit from the fridge and began cutting it up. She left the bar and a few minutes later my manager Zoe walked in.

'Put down the knife' she said.

'Why'? I asked without looking at her. She walked up to me, took the knife from my hand, and turned me around to face her.

'Because you're not working tonight'. I stepped back and told her she were crazy. I went to pick the knife up again but she got to it first, so I turned around and started setting the bar mats out. 'Lux you are not working tonight' she said again. 'Look at you! Look at your face! I cannot have you working a bar tonight! The punters cannot see you like this! You are coming round the back and sitting with me' she sternly told me.

'No, I'm not! I'm fine! I'm here to work'! I shouted back.

'Look at you! Look at your face'! She pointed to the mirrors behind the optics. I turned around and looked at myself. I was a bloody mess. My face was badly scratched and beating, my left eye beginning to swell shut. There was blood trickling its way down my cheek from a cut I hadn't felt above my right eye. There were red welts around my neck, and it wasn't until I saw my face that I felt any pain. I wrapped my arms around my stomach, trying to hold myself up as I let the pain take control.

I continued to stand there, with blood, bruising and swelling on my face and body and still repeated to her that I was fine. 'I'm here to work so I'm staying' I said again. With tears in her eyes, she gently took my hands and told me I was not working tonight. I was told I would go around back with her and she would keep me safe throughout my shift. I didn't understand this as I was already safe. The beating was over and I was fine, I didn't need anyone now. All I needed were a few painkillers and I had enough of those in my handbag. I marched off the bar, picked up my bag and started to walk towards the fire exit door. 'Where are you going'? Asked Zoe.

'If I'm not allowed to work a bar then I'm going home' I told her. She put her hand on my shoulder, guided me to the back and we sat down at the desk. She tried asking what happened, pleaded with me to tell her, and asked me to contact the police. I didn't. Instead, I made the decision that I would hand in my notice and leave.

***

For the next few years things calmed down. I would still get visits, texts, and calls but there could be months between each. It wasn't constant and I felt like I could drop my guard a little.

Only when things started to calm down and I had time to myself did I ever really fall apart. Why is that? I started having panic attacks which would render me on the floor. I couldn't be alone, I always needed someone there or someone on the phone with me. I ate as little as possible so I wouldn't have to go food shopping. I cancelled every plan I made with friends and gave the excuse I was called into work.

I did every minute of overtime I could. I barely ate, I barely slept, I lived on coffee, energy drinks, energy sweets and ProPlus. I was fainting all the time and I refused to speak with anyone. 'I'm fine' I would tell anyone who asked. Always the same lie.

In the call centre I shared a desk with my operations manager Sarah. Not many people on the floor liked Sarah but I think she was just misunderstood. She was opinionated, straight talking, and you always knew exactly where you stood with her. If something wasn't done, she would approach you and ask why; but that was her job, to make sure the people below her were doing their job and that tasks were being completed. She was also very funny and once you cracked that hard shell you found a warm and loving person underneath.

I had returned to my desk one morning and sat down when Sarah spoke 'I want to refer you for counselling. It's a 6-week programme and I really want you to try it. No-one else will know, after each session I get a report which tells me if you showed up but everything you discuss is confidential'.

I sat there for a few minutes looking at her. I was so confused. Nothing had happened recently. I hadn't received any visits; I wasn't covering up marks on my skin and I thought I had been acting pretty positive for a change. If I didn't need to bare my soul to a strange before then I definitely didn't need to do it now. But as I looked at Sarah I could see the worry in her eyes.

'I know you're concerned. I can see it. But I am okay. Everything will be fine now, I promise' I told her.

'Just have one session and see how it goes, it's good to talk with someone sometimes' Sarah pleaded with me. I could feel that sensation starting in the pit of my stomach again, trying to suppress the angry I could feel rising to the top. I didn't want to speak with anyone. I didn't want Sarah to worry. I didn't want to have to deal with any of this anymore. I was exhausted from it all. I let out a sigh.

'Okay I'll try it, for you'.

The appointment was made and I had every intention of giving it a chance, I really did. But as I took a seat on one of the old blue couches and the counsellor opened her notebook, looked at me and said, 'So what brings you here today', I knew counselling wasn't for me.

How was this person, however well-educated she may be, be able to help me work through years of torment in just 6-weeks? It was never going to happen.

So, I took a deep breath, changed my mask to my confident one, smiled and talked about every single other thing that was possibly going on in my life at that time. And the following five sessions went exactly the same. 'Yeah, I'm fine! Had a great day! This little thing happened the other day and this is how it made me feel, can you help me understand it'?

Not long after I completed the counselling course, my work advised us they were looking for people who would be interested in voluntary redundancy. I loved my job. I loved my team. I loved my work. I had a great deal of knowledge after working in almost every department over the past eight years and when I first read the email I causally laughed before deleting it.

A week later, I had been to get a coffee from the canteen where two different people asked me how I was. 'Fine thanks' I lied. I was so tired of people asking me that question. I returned to my desk and my team were talking about the voluntary redundancies, asking each other if they were applying for it. Someone asked me and the others laughed 'You'll have to take her out of here in a body bag, only way she would miss a day of work'. I smiled. But what she said was true and hit a nerve.

That day I decided it was time to leave. I had to get away from the stares, the chatter behind my back, the constant questions. I knew most people were concerned, but I couldn't take it anymore so I did what I do best and I ran. I applied for voluntary redundancy and had many conversations with different people in the workplace asking if I were sure I was making the right decision, did I need more time to think about it, informing me there would be another voluntary redundancy sent out next year and would I wait until then to apply. I thanked everyone for their concerns, confirmed I was sure I knew what I was doing and in time it was authorised.

It was a scary place to be. I had a clean slate to start somewhere new, where no-one knew my background and I could be anyone and anything I wanted to be.

Chapter Ten

After my six-week counselling hadn't quite gone to plan, Sarah asked if I would attend a support group. 'I'll help you find one and I'll come with you if you need me to'. I knew she meant it but I couldn't drag someone into my crazy world. I couldn't have what happened to me be put in her head. All the pain, the mistakes, the truth about what really happened, I couldn't do that to someone else.

'That's very kind of you, maybe one day I'll look into that' I told her.

'If you don't want to go to a support group, I'm sure you'll be able to look one up online. I really think it's something that would help, having people who've gone through similar experiences to talk with'. Sarah didn't know what had happened to me, or what was continuing to happen but she knew I was struggling and she knew there was nothing she personally could do to help me.

I hated that name, 'support group'. I didn't need support and I had no right to seek it. What happened to me, I let it happen. Everything else that followed, that was my fault too. I had numerous times throughout my life where all I had to do was open my mouth and tell the person standing in front of me, but I didn't. I didn't deserve to infringe on other people's healing. I was a phony.

I was on the bus heading home from work a few nights later and decided to look online, just to see if there was anything out there, to see if there were people who could relate, even a little, to what had happened to me. Maybe there was someone I could help?

I wasn't sure what to search. After a few minutes of staring blankly at the blinking cursor on my screen, my fingers cautiously started to type 'online support group for abuse'. Abuse, it made me laugh. I wasn't a battered wife; I didn't have parents who beat me or a partner who was keeping me locked away from the outside world. 'This is pointless' I told myself.

The first few searches to come up were helpline numbers and online counselling groups. I didn't need those. I kept scrolling. I stopped when I saw a description that caught my eye. 'This is a site for survivors of abuse. This is a supportive place where survivors can meet one another' It read. Survivors? I'm not a survivor, but I couldn't help reading and re-reading the description 'supportive place where survivors can meet one another'. I clicked the link and it opened a webpage. 'Working together and moving forward. Dedicated to survivors of rape and abuse'. It even had an inspirational video to go with its description.

I clicked on the community tab at the top of the screen where the words 'create an account' were staring back at me. Did I really want to do this? I didn't feel like I needed help plus everything that happened to me, I had let happen. I didn't deserve to now ask for help. 'What's the harm in looking' the voice in my head spoke up.

I slowly started to type. It didn't ask for an email address, just a username. I decided if I was doing this then I was going to be me. I typed in my name, 'username already taken'. I re-typed my name and added a few numbers to the end of it. This username was not taken. 'Okay, half-way there' that voice told me. I set up a password and clicked the big red button 'CREATE ACCOUNT'.

The site had message boards, different topics you could talk about. You could post things publicly for everyone to read or post things privately on your own page. There was a welcome page where every new member could tell something about themselves, and a place you could ask questions you didn't know the answers to. You could post fictional stories, another place where you could post poems and thoughts. There were different chat rooms: ones for general talk, others for topics of a more sensitive nature. I didn't know it then but this site was about to take over my life.

Reading other people's stories, talking with them when they were so low and didn't have anyone else to listen; kids who were posting from school saying they didn't want to go home; men, women, it just broke my heart. I logged onto that site every day to see if there was anyone needing help. I commented on every new post that was made. I welcomed every new member who joined. I would sit for hours in chat rooms talking with people who were just having a bad day. It didn't make what happened to me less difficult to deal with, but it did make me feel better that there were people who could relate a little. It made it easier to deal with things that had happened. When I recognised the pain of others, I felt less alone. It were as though we were all in this torment together.

I would always feel like a hypocrite though, telling people it wasn't their fault, they did nothing wrong, trying to get them to open up and telling them talking would help. Trying to convince people to go to their GP for help with anxiety or sleeping or to ask for a referral to counselling. The whole time I barely spoke about me or what had happened but I didn't feel I needed to, I felt better trying to help everyone else.

Since joining the site, I posted publicly four times. Everyone was kind and everyone had their own story. Even when they themselves were feeling self-despair, hopelessness, and desperation, they would still show up to support others. What amazing people they were.

I would be sitting in work or doing something around the house, I would be with family and friends or lying-in bed at night thinking 'I just have to check in case someone is reaching out, sending a private message and I'm not there'.

It became my addiction. After doing this for about two years I took a step back and realised I couldn't continue doing what I was doing. I wasn't sleeping, I couldn't concentrate on anything else, my mind was consumed with thinking about other people's pain at that exact moment. All different people from around the world in all different situations, all hurting and lonely.

It was one the toughest decisions of my life at that time. I rarely did anything for myself, but even I knew I couldn't keep this up. It took up ninety percent of my time thinking about it, wondering, worrying. I could not do it anymore.

So, with a heavy heart and tears streaming down my face I logged onto the site. I couldn't just abandon the people who had come to rely on me, people I had built relationships with so I sent them a private message explaining how I was feeling. I had already made up a new email address and passed this onto each one. I told them if they ever needed to chat, a safe place, a listening ear or just someone who saw them and not just their story, that I would always be here.

I still visit the site every now and then, chat with new members via the welcome board, visit the chat rooms. Some of the people I used to chat with are still there and it warms my heart to hear how good they are doing, the changes they had the strength to make in their own lives. Taking a step back was the right decision for me.

<u>Posted October 7, 2012</u>

I've never done this chat room thing before, not really sure how it works. I'm 27 and now after everything has slowed down, I feel like my world has turned upside down which is strange because I was fine when everything was going on. Anyway, I found this site last night and it was just what I needed, everyone seems nice and everyone can relate which is scary but good too. I've never done counselling and my family have no idea what went on for years, but everyone needs to start somewhere I guess

Posted June 6, 2013

Tomorrow we have to bury my cousin and the whole day should be about him and how his life has been cut short, about the amazing person he was and I'm going to do everything I can to keep it that way

I've just been speaking with his sister who said 2, possibly 3, of his old mates from high school will be there. These guys are part of the reason why I'm here on this site and none of my family know about that. I haven't seen any of them in 10 months and last time I did it didn't end well. I didn't even know they knew my cousin until tonight!

I have to be there tomorrow for my family but I'm so scared that seeing them again will bring back things that I know I haven't dealt with and what if it all starts again? I couldn't handle that and there's no-one I can tell, and my mind is racing and my heart is pounding right now and I don't know what to do

Posted February 19, 2014

I can't believe I'm saying this, but it's been 14 years today since it all started, since he held me down & the light in my soul went out. Where has the time gone? I was 14 at the time, I've spent exactly half of my life living with this. What?!? That sounds so crazy!

My family don't know, I've never said it out loud & I never talk about it. For years I put it out of my head because for years after that night he would show up at school, college, work, my home, he'd be on his own or have friends with him, I've had my wrists broken, black eyes, broken ribs, knife cuts, cigarette burns. He would sit outside my house in a car for hours some days with his friends and just look at my house but he wouldn't get out the car. I took driving lessons once, but I never sat my test because I was afraid they would mess with the breaks and afraid of passing and just getting in my car and disappearing because how could I explain that to everyone? Plus, I had no-where to go

He's dead now, he died in a car accident 4 years ago & that's when I started falling apart, after it had finished, and I thought I was free THEN I started to fall apart. I've never worked this day ever, not sure why, it's not like it's any different to any other day, it's not like he's coming back from the grave to get me, he's dead but once a year no matter how good I'm doing or how bad I'm doing I dread this day. I'm so glad it's almost over so tomorrow can be normal again.

I've never had a long-term boyfriend, I've never allowed myself to fall in love because to love someone you need to know them & how could someone love me & not know what happened? I could never tell them; I could never trust them with my secret. Why is it a secret? I didn't ask him to do any of it, I did everything they asked me to, I learned early on it was pointless to fight back, maybe I should have fought harder.

Anyway, here I am, 14 years on & even though I got through school and college and had different jobs and lived in different places it's like my life has been on hold waiting for something but I don't know what it is and I'm getting a little tired of it. I want to travel, I want to pass my driving test, I want to work with people who have gone through what I have, people who were abused, children who were hurt, adults who are still trying to get their head around what happened to them but how can I do that? How can I sit with people and tell them it's going to be okay, that's its right to talk about it, to go to the police, to try things that scare them when I've never done any of it?

Posted January 12, 2019

So, I started counselling today. I briefly tried before a few years ago but I just couldn't do it and I didn't like it. I hated being in a room with 1 other person who was sitting there judging you

But the nightmares are back & worse than even. After 18 years I almost told my aunt what happened to me, we were out having dinner, just the 2 of us and the words almost came out but didn't. It was sitting with her and wanting to tell her that made me book a counselling session

Right now, half of me thinks 'wow go you really glad you're doing this & facing things' & the other half of me is thinking 'what did you just do, what's the point in counselling now after all this time? You've never been able to say the words out loud before so why would now be any different?'

My next session is a week today & I'll go to it, just worried & scared about remembering things, thoughts, feelings, places, faces but right now I don't feel like I'm living my life so what do I have to lose really. Maybe it is time to get over this

Chapter Eleven

My second attempt at counselling, my first real try, did not work out. I hated sitting in that room. The room was located at a main door and anytime anyone entered or exited the noise echoed around the four walls. There was a coloured sofa that we never used, a small wooden coffee table with a little white clock on it, two comfortable chairs facing each other, a fireplace on the opposite end of the room from the door and huge windows facing onto the carpark. The windows were mostly covered by thick dark curtains and white netting but I couldn't help feeling as though I were being watched as I sat in that chair.

The counsellor was a lady in her 50's; she had short grey hair and a warm smile. She asked what brought me there, and I told her some of my reasons. I didn't only need help with the parts of my life consumed by Alex and his friends, but also with family matters and my work.

I don't trust easily; I can get a vibe within minutes of meeting someone new and I know exactly what mask I need to wear around them. I'm not someone who listens to other people's opinions on someone I've yet to meet either; I take their thoughts and emotions into account and wait until I meet that person for myself before drawing my own conclusions on who they are.

Sitting in this old, cold room I could see that she was trying to make me comfortable. Having a bottle of water ready when I came in, making the lighting soft, having the two chairs spaced far enough apart but not too far, and using gentle tones. None of it helped, all I thought about was the next time the door would slam or if people outside could hear me as clearly as I could hear them. My mind spent more time looking out the window into the carpark waiting to see if anyone I knew passed rather than concentrating on what was going on inside the room.

I did not feel comfortable sitting with another stranger staring at me, writing down every second word I said. How could she concentrate on what I was saying if she spent fifty percent of the time writing? I didn't feel as though I could open up and speak about the things that had happened. I spent most of the time talking about different things within my family that were worrying me and about my work as I was struggling to decide what I wanted to do next with my career.

She knew I were there looking for help with more than one issue but anytime I tried to talk about something else, she would always tell me I wouldn't move past 'it' if I didn't talk about 'it' and I felt I was wasting both our time. She was pressuring me into diving right in and talking about the most horrific things that had ever happened to me and just expecting it were easy for me to talk about. She was a counsellor; didn't she know how difficult that was?

Maybe if she had spent more time allowing me to talk about other things and become comfortable with her, I would have eventually opened up more. I remember her telling me once that on the rare occasion I did touch on why I was really there, that I had no emotion and it were as though I was talking about something that had happened to someone else. That made sense to me.

I had always felt, and sometimes continue to feel like there is this other person inside me, the one who all the bad things happened to. It didn't happen to me, it happened to her. If I feel a panic attack coming on or if the nightmares get bad again, I always push it away, push it down like I'm scared of letting that part of me out because I have no idea what that side of me would look like. It's easier to think of these things happening to someone else rather than myself. I try not to think of what that other part of me looks like; being kept in a box all these years with the memories, heartache, pain, the road map of trauma covering her entire body, all alone in the dark for so many years. She may be locked up but she's safer there than coming out into the light and trying to live.

It's bad enough living with the recurring memories I do have, and I know there are many more I don't, and having to battle them daily. Distant memories: things that come back and knock the wind out of me, the ones that are triggered by things going on around me, those memories I did not need or want to deal with. My entire body continues to freeze whenever I smell Cool Waters aftershave or see a male wearing a white jumper and my head automatically jumps right back to those moments. I can vividly see where I am, hear what's going on around me, feel his hands on me and all I can do is wait for it to pass. It's my own private hell.

The counsellor sat me down one session and began explaining PTSD to me. 'Post-traumatic stress disorder is a condition caused by a traumatic experience' she started. I knew this, I had learned about it in English years before after reading a poem entitled 'Dulce et Decorum est Pro patria mori'. 'You have all the symptoms of PTSD' she went on. 'In my opinion, you have PTSD' she finished.

I sat there, dumfounded. Had I heard her correctly? Me? Have PTSD? That was ridiculous. I didn't have PTSD. Yes bad things had happened in my life but bad things happen in everyone's life and throwing PTSD around like that, in my opinion, was downright dangerous. Maybe I should have checked her credentials before I arranged a session. More fool me eh? She had probably flicked through a few books in a library one time and made up everything else. I didn't have PTSD. I was fine.

'Thank you for your opinion on this matter' I kindly said with a half-smile as I rose, picked up my coat, opened the huge heavy door and made my way across the gravel carpark. I never went back.

As I left, I realised I couldn't control what happened that night with Alex. I couldn't control when he showed up, what he did. I couldn't control the calls or texts or his friends taking over when he died. I couldn't control any of those things, but that didn't give me the right to ask for help now. I didn't deserve it.

Yes, I couldn't control what happened to me, but I could have easily opened my mouth and told someone years before.

I could have walked into my aunt and uncles living room that night and told them what he had just done to me. I could have walked into my house and told my dad that first time I got in his car and he drove me home, or any of the other times it happened. I could have reached out to any one of my teachers who were begging me to speak with them. I could have told the police when they were called to my work, but I didn't. I kept silent and it kept happening. Living with this was my eternal punishment.

I stayed quiet about everything and it kept happening. How dare I have the right to tell anyone I'm struggling now? If only I had opened my mouth then, I wouldn't still be dealing with it all now. I knew this to be true. I didn't need to open up to someone else and have them tell me it was my fault or sigh and ask why I never told anyone. I am harder on myself than anyone else could ever be.

At times in my life, I feel as though so much control has been taken away from me that I cling to anything and everything I can control. If I make a plan and it doesn't go exactly as I thought it would, I become anxious. If life throws me a curveball that I wasn't ready for, I struggle to deal with it. Over the years I've had to trick my brain into thinking I'm ready for anything. And if something unexpected happens, I jump right into action before the fear and panic have time to take over. It's exhausting. But that's what keeps me feeling safe.

I had never been in a serious relationship. To love someone, you must know them. All of them. Their wishes and desires, their hopes, dreams, the good, bad and the ugly. I could never tell anyone my secrets; no-one could ever truly love me if they knew what had happened to me, the things I had done, so what was the point in damaging them with my poison.

After that first night I told myself I was fine and for years after I threw myself at anyone who would have me. I would have sex with anyone; it didn't matter if it were a guy from school in the bathroom, a friend of a friend I had never met before, some random guy I bumped into at a bar or a lecturer at college in the back of his car. I didn't care. I didn't feel anything towards them. These guys were not looking for love, they didn't want a girlfriend. They wanted to fuck someone who would say as little as possible then walk away feeling like a champion once they were finished. And that's exactly where I fit in. I was being used and I liked it. It was safe to me because it was on my terms.

If any relationship started to feel like it were getting a little too comfortable or real, I would end it. If they asked where my scars came from or if I was out with them and happened to run into Alex or his friends and they saw the guy I was with, I would end it because I couldn't risk anything happening to them because of me.

I moved out when I was 21 and I never lived alone. I lived with friends, colleagues, family of friends, strangers. I never lived with a boyfriend. Yes, I would spend most of my time with them, but I always had someplace to call home for those times when I needed a break or when they told me they were sick of me and threw me out for a few days then would come back begging me to forgive them and go back, which I always did. This merry-go-round of abusive relationships lasted years. I didn't have any self-worth. I had no self-respect so why did it matter if anyone else had it for me? I was never going to be someone special or accomplish great things. I was only good for one thing, keeping my legs open, my mouth shut, lying there taking it then waiting to be thrown away like the trash I felt I was.

It didn't matter who I lived with, I felt safer just living with someone, anyone. I never worried about the people I lived with; they were never in any danger. I was the one they wanted, they weren't stupid enough to bring anyone else into it now and risk them being braver than I ever was. Living alone scared me more than living with strangers. If Alex had flowers delivered to my home, if they sat outside watching me when they knew I were not alone, whenever they drove me home and didn't walk me to the door as they could clearly see someone else was home, then would that all change if they knew there was no-one on the other side of that door? Absolutely it would, there was no doubt in my mind of that.

Chapter Twelve

When I left the energy company, I took a few months off and tried to decide what I wanted to do with my life. I knew I was running away again, away from the stares and the whispers but what if I were running to something better? It was foolish to leave but I had to and leaving took courage too did it not? I felt overloaded, exhausted, and running was the only thing I knew how to do. And by then I had become a master at it.

But what was I good at? Not very much to be honest. Did I have any passions? Not really. I had always wanted to travel, even signed up for a gap year abroad when I was 21 but things happened and I never went. Maybe I could travel now? I certainly had enough saved up in the bank to do so. Where would I go? Would I do a year in Australia like I planned when I was 21? Would I backpack around the states like I saw so many do on TV? What about the 7 wonders of the world, surely that would somehow help fill the emptiness in me. Would they follow me if I left? I highly doubted that but never say never.

My favourite TV programme has always been Law & Order SVU and I often watch it on repeat. I love how the episodes start off with the crime, then the police get involved, the person attacked finds the strength to tell their truth, it goes to trial and in the end the bad guy is locked up. I know real life is nothing like this, but still, it is a nice thought. The show hasn't run for as many years as it has because no-one could be bothered taking if off the air; it has run for so long because it is the only show that speaks about this type of abuse and shows it from all angles. People who didn't have an outlet, who didn't have support, could watch the show, and feel like someone cared. That good could win. That all bad things can come to an end eventually.

A lot of the episodes are based on real events and when I'm having a bad day, whether the nightmares or the flashbacks or the memories creep back in, I will turn on SVU, sometimes watching it for days on end and remind myself that good can win. This has helped lift me from the dark hole I've creeped back inside of and brought me out into the light. Knowing I am not alone, that there are people in the world who have gone through, in some form or another, what I have, and worse, it helps.

The idea of working with people affected by sexual assault, domestic violence and child abuse had been circling my brain for the last couple of years. It was something I wanted to do, but something I never thought I could. How could I help anyone? I had never taken any help offered to me. I didn't have any wisdom to part onto others, couldn't explain what would happen if they went to the police or how that would feel. I couldn't do any of those things. I would just be a burden in their healing and people who had been abused needed strength and guidance in their corner, not a hypocrite.

But the thought would not leave my mind. It had wormed its way into my brain and spread like cancer, clinging on to anything it touched. Maybe I could do this. I'm sure I would get training before they let me speak with people who needed my help.

I thought if I at least dipped my toes into the water, I could get a feel for things. I looked up support services near me, and a few that weren't so close. I emailed every organisation I could find, asking if they were hiring or looking for volunteers but I could find nothing. Emails came back undelivered or filled with thanks and promises to keep my name on a waiting list. I was broken hearted. I had finally found a passion and felt as though the universe were sending me a sign saying I wasn't good enough. It wasn't wrong.

I began to look up care jobs online, hoping to find something and found so many applications for care staff. This was something I had never thought about and it was so far from what I now wanted to do but at least it was working in care. Maybe it would give me some sort of experience that would be helpful, and if I could help people along the way, that surely was a bonus.

I went to a jobs fair for a company who supported vulnerable adults living at home. I listened to their speeches, watched their videos, asked the staff questions and by the end of the day I had filled in an application form. It still wasn't what I wanted to do but after spending the day listening to the staff and some residents, I started getting a feeling in the pit of my stomach that this may not be what I wanted to do but was rather something I was supposed to do.

The following week I started my training and by the end of the second week I was absolutely in love with my new job. I was genuinely helping people and it felt great! We supported vulnerable adults with everyday tasks, everything from getting up in the morning until going to bed at night. People who had no family, only us to depend on and take care of them. People who didn't have a voice and needed us to speak for them. This wasn't just a job to me. To me, this was one of the most important jobs I could ever have the privilege of doing.

I loved working in care. I loved the people I cared for. I loved taking them on outings, going shopping, stopping for lunch or dinner, seeing their whole face light up when they smiled because of something you had done. Going into work on a sunny say and deciding together to take a drive somewhere nice, by the water. Watching as they tried new things and enjoyed them. Being there during the good times and the bad, guiding them to make their own choices and making sure they were heard, even if they couldn't communicate this themselves. It truly warmed my heart.

I worked so many hours and I never did it for the money, the money was not that great and I rarely had time off to spend what I did make. I didn't do it for the company or the management, I did it because I knew if the shifts weren't covered then the people I cared for would miss out on something that day, that for that day they wouldn't receive the level of care they so deserved, and that was not going to happen. Not on my watch. I put my whole heart and soul into my job and couldn't understand why others in the same job role didn't do the same. It frustrated me to watch people who had been in the job for years forget that there was an actual person standing in front of them and not someone who had to be told what to do and have all their decisions made for them instead of with them. It broke my heart. Giving my best every day and trying to make up for the shortfall of others, it took its toll on me and in the end I couldn't do it anymore. It took everything I had and I had to leave.

Deciding to leave that job was one of the hardest decisions of my life. Sitting here years later I still go over it in my head, asking myself if I did the right thing. Feeling guilty about not staying longer. Missing the people I cared for and wanting to go back, even just for one day to see their faces, hear their laughter once more.

Whilst working there I met some interesting people. Some I thought couldn't care properly for themselves and shouldn't be in the job, others who put everything they had into everything they did.

I met two strangers. Strangers who became friends. Friends who became family. They were, and continue to be, my calm in this crazy storm of life. When I think of them I think of that William Shakespeare quote 'a friend is one that knows you as you are, understands where you have been, accepts what you have become, and still, gently allows you to grow'. Most people in my life only saw the daily mask I wore upon my face; Tink and Lexi saw straight through the mask to my fractured heart, my shattered soul.

They are always there, even to this day. If their own lives are throwing fiery curveballs at them, they will always show up, lend a helping hand, offer words of support and comfort. Sometimes, just talking with them about nothing is all the therapy I need. I could have never made it to this place in my life without the two of them being my own personal cheerleaders. I often wonder why they stick around; I can be hard work at the best times, but I've slowly come to realise it's because they genuinely care about me and that feels good.

My family were not there when I needed them to be; when I walked through my aunt and uncle's door that night and had marks that falling on ice wouldn't cause, when my mother found what I had written and threw it back in my face, when she had been called so many times to school and acted like I was bothering her. When my dad spent the afternoon building a hut with him and seeing me sitting on the step, not moving, not speaking, shaking in fear of what Alex may do or say. My family may not have been there but Tink and Lexi were, they were always right there by my side. We have an agreement to never use the word 'fine' as this is usually not true and also to tell each other when we're bleeding internally so the other two can show up and help.

We have had our friendship tested by envious people which only resulted in making our bond stronger. We have each separately been through hell and back, we know each other's secrets and I love them both unconditionally. Being around them is like holding onto a big steaming mug of hot tea, they always warm my heart.

They opened a world filled with quotes that accurately described what I felt when my own mind couldn't find the words and introduced me to songs that could have been sang directly from my heart.

These quotes and song lyrics were not always filled with positivity and light, they were dark and twisty but they spoke directly to me and they helped. Putting my headphones in, turning the volume as high as possible and letting someone else scream the words that I had hidden inside for so long, it was my own course of therapy.

I created a private page where I could store all the quotes and I set up playlists for the songs that could have come from my own heart. Even though the words and lyrics were dark and painful, they would somehow help me to feel better. I can't explain this. Maybe it was finally having the words to describe what was in my heart and mind that really helped me.

Even with the support of my friends and music therapy, I still had bad days. I would shut down, shut off from the world. I would go to work, put all my energy into doing the best job I could then I would come home and crash. I would be silent; I wouldn't make or answer calls and messages. I would get lost in my own memories. Not wanting to die, but not quite wanting to live my life either. I remember Tink saying this thing to me once, that she wouldn't do anything to end her life but if a car were coming straight towards her, she wouldn't necessarily move out of the way either.

At first I really didn't understand this. It scared me that someone could feel so low that this would be a thought for them. As time passed, however, I understood that statement all too well. I wouldn't take steps to end my life but if it happened through natural causes or someone else's mistake, then that would be okay with me.

The girls always knew when I was hiding from reality. They would give me space, sometimes sending a quick message of support, letting me know they were just a call or text away. If I hadn't managed to pull myself out of the darkness within a few days, they were right there telling me it was okay to feel the way I were feeling but that I couldn't live there forever and together they would pull me out.

My response to locking myself away, to reading quotes repeatedly and listening to lyrics that made me remember more than I wanted to, shutting everyone out, it was not healthy. I knew this; however, this is what I had always done. Closing down had kept me safe, kept me sane. And it had gotten me this far, so could it really be all that bad?

Chapter Thirteen

A couple of years ago, I started seeing a guy named Josh. We had first met online and within one week met in person. Josh was bald and had a beard, he had that rugged look, his shoulders were broad, his arms were strong and his green eyes would sparkle when the sun hit them at the right angle. Josh was taller than I and whenever he wrapped his strong arms around me, for a few seconds, I felt safe.

Josh was funny; he made me laugh all the time with his jokes and impressions of different famous people. He would goof around doing silly dances, play harmless practical jokes on me, and poke fun at himself too. He could be a little cocky at times but it was harmless, at first.

And his greatest love was food. He would spend a lot of time online sourcing different places to eat, speaking with the chefs and asking what new meals were on the menu. He would get tips on how to cook any type of meat and what drinks complimented each dish. He would spend hours reading through recipes taking a little from this and a little from that to make his own masterpieces. Watching Josh cook was mesmerising, he would get lost in the recipes, the colours, the spices, the different flavourings. He treated each dish with such delicacy and care it was hard not to fall for him.

Josh would get so excited when he found a 'diamond in the rough' as he called them. He would confer with the chefs to know when they were working then we would go along and try new dishes, some even made us dishes that weren't available on the menu and Josh adored this. He would sit at the table and smile as though he were King. The chefs would come out afterwards and ask how the food was and Josh loved this; he would give his unbiased opinion telling the chef what he liked, what he didn't and what he thought could make each dish better. He would listen intently to what each chef taught him in the few minutes they spent with us. His eyes would grow wide and he would take notes in his phone of different methods to try and would question chefs if two told him different ways of cook something.

I never joined in on the conversations with chefs. I enjoyed watching him as he became excited talking about spices, different cuts of meat, vegetables, cooking temperatures, different ways to cook food. He was like a child at Christmas in a toy store.

It didn't matter whether we were sitting in a bar eating food on a table that had so many bumps and scratches in it that it was hard to think of it as once being new, or if we were in a fancy restaurant that sparkled with waiters who literally bowed at the table, he always spoke to each chef the same way and gave his opinions. He was a very straight talker.

Josh had been speaking to a certain chef online one week who told us to come along the following weekend and he would make us up a special dish that wasn't on the menu.

The restaurant was nice. It wasn't fancy, its décor was old, the tables were dark brown and the windows had curtains that looked as though they had never been taken down and washed since the day they were put up. But it did have big windows that let in a lot of light; the bar looked as though it had just been refurbished with new bar stools, sparkling optics, and bar mats with the restaurant's name on them.

We were seated half-way between the bar and the huge windows when the waiter approached us and asked for our drinks order.

'I'm here to see Mark, he's expecting me' Josh told her nonchalantly. Presumably expecting that the waiter would run directly to the kitchen and tell the head chef that he had an important visitor.

'I'm sorry, do you mean Mark the bar manager or Mark the chef' the waiter politely asked.

'Why would I be here to see a bar manager'? Josh stated a smirk on his face and a little frustration rising in his voice.

'Oh, Mark the chef is not working today' she gracefully divulged. There was a flash in Josh's eyes that I had never seen before. The waitress saw it too and she kept going 'I mean, he was supposed to be working the dinner shift but he called in sick this morning' she hurriedly explained.

'Why the hell didn't he let me know'? Josh was becoming increasingly frustrated. 'I came all the way here because Mark told me he would be working and would make me something that wasn't on the damn menu', his voice getting louder.

'I'm so sorry, let me go speak with the chef and see if Mark mentioned anything, maybe the chef could make you something special' she tried to diffuse the situation.

'I did not come here to waste my time tasting food from an amateur chef, I came here because Mark told me he would be here and would make me a special dish'. Josh's tone was changing. His rising voice had caught the attention of some other customers sitting nearby and of the manager who came straight over.

'Is there a problem sir'? He politely enquired.

'A problem'? Josh sneered. 'You are the one with the problem mate, having amateur staff working here who wouldn't know a good cut of steak from a raw chicken breast and I've just wasted my time getting a train and walking 20 minutes to get here' Josh said angrily, his face beginning to contort with rage, his jaw clenching, his nostrils flaring. I was more than a little taken aback by his behaviour as I had never seen this side to him. I jumped into action and tried to calm him down.

'It's okay Josh, we can order something from the menu. You said the reviews were really good and I'm sure Mark doesn't work all the shifts. I bet the other chef is pretty good too' I tried to reason with him. I put my hand on his arm but he violently pushed me away.

'I didn't come all this way to be insulted by a cocky arrogant prick who can't cook' he told me, not taking his eyes off the manager. I couldn't understand why he was so angry. Yes, it took us a while to get here, but the reviews had been great and there was plenty on the menu for us to choose from.

'Sir, if you don't calm down I am going to have to ask you to leave' the manager sternly told him.

'You're throwing *me* out? Why the hell do you think I would want to sit here and eat anything you served'? Josh replied. He got up, picked up his jacket and headed towards the door. For a second I thought he had genuinely forgot I was there until he turned around and told me we were leaving and wouldn't be back.

'I'm sorry, he's having a difficult time right now' I lied to the staff. Josh heard this and came pounding towards me. He grabbed my left arm, pulling me close to him and looked me straight in the eyes.

'What the hell did you just say'? He shouted at me. 'No-one apologises for me'! I was told. I was shocked by his actions and said nothing else as he dragged me across the floor. There was a tray of dirty glasses sitting at the edge of the bar and as we passed Josh pushed it hard, causing the glasses to fall and shatter as they hit the tiled floor. He didn't stop and was pulling the door open as I heard the manager talk to the waitress.

'It's okay, you handled that well. He's just a jock who's used to getting his own way'. I prayed that his words wouldn't reach Josh's ears as I feared what would happen if they did, but he didn't appear to have been listening.

'Where are we going' I asked once we were outside. No answer. 'Josh let go of my arm'. He let go but didn't answer me. 'Josh talk to me! What the hell was that all about back there'? I yelled at him. He stopped, turned on his heels and took a step towards me. For a second I thought he was going to hit me and I embraced myself for whatever blow he gave, but he didn't raise his hands.

'What the hell is wrong with you? You didn't say a word in there when that incompetent jack-ass was insulting me. You're fucking useless' he fiercely spat at me then abruptly turned around and walked away. I stood there, my whole body shaking, my mind racing. Had I missed something at the restaurant? Did the staff insult him and I hadn't noticed it? In my opinion no, they had not.

I did not want to be around him right now so I headed for the nearest bus stop and went home alone. I never told anyone about his outburst., somehow I felt embarrassed about it, like I was the one in the wrong.

A familiar feeling was starting to stir in the pit of my stomach. I had had a front row seat and witnesses both sides to Josh; as much as he could be kind and gentle, he could me bitter and nasty.

I had never been in a relationship that wasn't stormy and I was beginning to get a little tired by it. I wasn't looking for prince charming to come galloping by on his valiant stallion, swoosh me up into his arms and take me to live happily ever after in his fairy-tale castle but was it too much to ask for someone who actually saw me? Was this my punishment for keeping quiet all these years? Having partners who thought me unworthy of joy or love? Who put me down instead of reaching out a supportive hand? Was I only fit to be demeaned, unsupported and attacked? Would I ever feel worthy? I was beginning to realise I was more lost than I had thought. I never allowed myself to show who I really was as I spent my time on edge, waiting on the next blow, the next tantrum and wondering what I could do to avoid it from happening before it was too late.

A few days later, Josh asked me to meet him. I was hesitant but said yes. We met for lunch and when I arrived he handed me the biggest bunch of flowers I had ever seen. The flowers were all different types but all yellow in colour, my favourite.

'I'm so sorry babe. I was having a shit day and really wanted to treat you to something special and I just lost it when Mark wasn't there. I sent him a message telling him he could shove his food up his own arsehole' he informed me. Then went on. 'But it's alright because I was talking to the chef in here last night and he said to come in and he would make us some pretty sick toasted sandwiches. He said we can have a side of anything we want. I told him we would have those fries we had last month, with the haggis, peppercorn sauce and grated cheese so he's making us that' he smiled, almost jumping for joy.

He looked so excited again. I had always been a laid-back person and was happy going with the flow. Don't get me wrong, if there was something I really didn't want to do or someplace I really didn't want to go or something I really didn't want to eat, I would firmly say no. But I liked a toasted sandwich. I didn't like haggis but that was okay because Josh ate the whole plateful last time so I knew he would do the same this time.   Sometimes I felt more like a dining companion than a girlfriend.   I wondered if he would even notice if I were to get up and leave.

Chapter Fourteen

The following weekend, Josh told me to meet him at 8am at the train station. When I arrived, he had a rucksack on his back and a small gift box in his hand. He kissed me on the cheek and told me to open the box. Inside was his bracelet that he never took off. I always played with it whenever we were sitting relaxing. It had little wooden beads on a string, nothing special but I liked it.

'What's this'? I asked.

'I know how much you love this and I wanted you to have something of mine for when I'm not there'. His eyes were sincere, pleading with mine to accept his gift.

'I love it, thank you' I replied.

'I love you. You know that right? I love you and I would never do anything to hurt you. I couldn't live without you'. He wrapped his arms tightly around me and kissed me. 'There's the Josh I know' I thought to myself. It was the first time he had used that word love. I knew I didn't love him back, and it was still early to be saying it to each other but he never looked for me to respond. He wouldn't tell me where we were going; he bought train tickets and we headed off. After the train ride, we hopped a ferry and finally stopped at this beautiful Island. The sun was starting to warm up, the smell from the water and freshly cut grass all around us was delicious. We stood at a little row of shops and I asked him which direction we were going in.

'You choose, today is your day' he surprised me by saying. I chose straight and we walked and walked and walked some more. The scenery was amazing and we stopped a few times to take photos along the way. We walked in old grounds that were so beautiful, mesmerising even. At lunchtime we sat down and had a picnic. He had everything - sandwiches, different meats, cheese, fruit, pasta, rice, cold snacks, coleslaw, wine, everything I could think of.

'I really do love you; you know. I'm sorry about the restaurant, I promise it won't happen again' he told me.

'It's okay, I know it won't' I said but didn't quite believe it. The rest of the day was just as great. We laughed, we watched seals bathing on rocks, we fed the birds and I began to relax around him again. Josh loved red wine. He would drink it every day and had brought some on our picnic. I didn't really like it, and he knew this, but it wasn't a big problem for me. Anywhere we went, he ordered it. He would always order my food and the drink he thought best compliment whatever dish he had chosen for me. He never ordered anything I didn't like. A few dishes were not great but I wouldn't have known that before trying them. The only thing I didn't like was seafood and he never ordered me seafood.

One night I had gone to a friends for dinner. Josh was out with his friends and I had no plans so when she asked me to come over I didn't hesitate in saying yes. We ordered pizza and watched a movie. Josh had called a few times and I told him where I was and what we were doing. He told us to have a good night and that he would see me in the morning. As the night went on, I was beginning to get more texts, more calls, more voicemails from Josh. I knew he was out drinking with friends but he was becoming angry with me. He had asked me to take a photo of the leftover pizza and send it to him. I was confused by this but thought if I did it then he would settle down for the night.

'What are you doing'? My friend asked.

'Oh nothing, Josh just asked me to send him a photo of our pizza' I explained. I knew it sounded strange but I was hoping she would laugh it off. She didn't.

'Please don't send him that photo' she said

'It's fine, it's just some pizza. Hopefully he'll leave us alone after this' I tried to reason with her.

'I'm asking you, please don't send that photo' she said again, more forcefully. Something in her eyes made me stop and put the phone down. She went on to explain how she got a bad vibe from Josh but hadn't known how to tell me because in the beginning I had seemed happy. She had noticed recently that things had changed and she was worried about me.

'He chooses where you go, what you do, who you hang out with, what you eat and what you drink. He even chooses what you wear sometimes! Lux, he's controlling you and it scares me' she tried to reason.

'He doesn't control me'! I tried to defend him. 'Yeah he chooses a lot of things but if I didn't want to go somewhere or eat something or wear something then I wouldn't do it.

You're blowing this way out of proportion' I told her. Things became quiet as we sat together in silence for a few minutes.

'Lux, please don't send that photo. I know you completely disagree with me right now and that's okay and I know you might be afraid of what happens next but I am right here. I will always have your back' she told me. I thought about her words. It was only a silly photo so why was she pushing this so much? I knew she was scared but I didn't understand why. Josh had never hit me. I wasn't afraid of him, was I? I wasn't sure what I felt. As I looked at my friend I saw the pain in her eyes. I realised it didn't matter what I thought but instead that she thought she was right and was genuinely concerned about me. I cautiously deleted the photo from my phone, took a deep breath and waited to see what would happen. It didn't take long for me to find out.

He text, then text again and then text some more. Then he started calling. I didn't answer. I knew he would be mad. I would be mad too if he was out and suddenly stopped replying to me. I thought 'it's fine, I'll apologise tomorrow or say we were having such a good time I didn't hear my phone'. My friend asked me if I wanted to spend the night, she was worried about me going back to Josh's house but I told her I would be fine and was going home instead. When I got home, I didn't dare read any of his messages or listen to his voicemails. Instead, I made myself a cup of tea, changed into my pyjamas, got into bed, and watched an episode of Charmed.

The next day I woke up to over 80 messages, missed calls and voicemails. Again, I didn't read or listen to any of them as I knew he was angry. Instead, I showered, dressed, and went to work as normal. We weren't allowed our phones in work and he knew this so I wasn't expecting anymore contact until I had finished work. When I got home I had a call from him, I cautiously answered.

'Think you're some big shot eh? Ignoring me and laughing about me behind my back to all your pals'? He asked. 'Where were you? Who were you with? What were you doing'? He went on.

'You know where I was, who I was with and what we were doing' I calmly responded. 'I was trying to enjoy my night and couldn't because of your constant messages so I put my phone on silent and put it into my bag' I explained. This seemed to enrage him. He started screaming at me, 'how dare I ignore him' and 'I was nothing but a whore'. He went on to tell me how stupid I was, how he was the only guy on the planet who would ever want me, that no-one showed him up in front of his mates. He was shouting and swearing at me for 20 minutes before I eventually ended the call. I sat there realising how right my friend had been. How could I have been so stupid? How had I not seen the signs? I knew he had a bit of a temper, had I seen it and not wanted to believe it or was I just that naive? Whatever the reason I now knew it was over. I sent him a text telling him no-one treats me that way, that I was nobody's fool and that it was over. Then I blocked his number.

A few months later he sent me a message from a different number saying he was sorry and asking to come over to my house. I was hesitant as I knew what he was like but he was so persistent. I replied saying I didn't want him in my home and he replied asking me to dinner. I didn't want to do that either because I had witnessed first-hand how he could be in a restaurant. I decided I would meet him, not at home, not in a restaurant and definitely not for drinks. I told him I was going shopping the next day and would give him 10 minutes.

When I met him, he had the biggest smile and looked so excited, he was almost jumping up and down. I had the same feeling I had when I first met him but I knew I couldn't go back there. I had to stand strong. He excitedly told me how he had been offered a job in Ireland and had looked at flats; he had found this nice one and was sure I would like it.

'You'll love it! It looks right onto the water' he told me. I wasn't sure exactly what he was meaning. Was he saying I could go visit or was he asking me to go live with him?

'That sounds nice' I told him. 'Are you wanting me to visit you'?

He looked at me strangely. I stared right back looking for him to elaborate. 'Visit me? No. You're coming with me! I've spoken to my boss and if he can't give you a job he'll help me look for something for you'. I was shocked. He was telling me he was moving to Ireland, that I was going with him, he had found us a place to live and he would find me a job? Any familiar feelings I had for him quickly turned. The feelings that followed were all too familiar.

'I'm not going to Ireland with you' I firmly but carefully told him. I watched his face for a hint of how he would react. He looked bewildered.

'Yes you are. We're going to Ireland. I've arranged it all. I found a place to live and I'm getting you a job. What else do you need'? He asked me.

My family. My friends. My job, I thought.

'Thank you for thinking of me, I appreciate it but I am not going to Ireland with you Josh' I said again. His eyes turned dark, I saw his jaw clench and I took a step back.

'You are coming to Ireland with me. I don't know what your problem is. I've arranged everything' he told me again.

'Josh, thank you but I am staying here. I'm not leaving my life and moving with you to a place I don't know, especially when we're not talking right now' I continued. I was angry but knew I had to remain cool or he would become angry too.

'Yes you are. You're not thinking straight. I'll give you a week to change your mind' he told me. 'I've got it all organised'.

I walked away and he stood there. I didn't turn around; I didn't ever want to see him again. After I had finished my shopping, I headed towards the bus station and found an empty seat. I was confident he wouldn't be around so I pulled out my phone and text his new number. 'I am not coming to Ireland. Hope things work out and you have a good life. Please don't contact me again'. Then I blocked that number too.

Chapter Fifteen

In my life, I've had two miscarriages. Neither of these pregnancies were planned. The first time I fell pregnant, I was seeing a guy named Dave. He was six years older than I and he could be a saint or a sinner. You never knew what side of him you would get. It didn't matter how he woke up as his mood would change drastically throughout the day.

Dave would either be obsessed with me, always wanting to know where I was, who I was with, what I was doing, how long I would be out or he would ignore me for days then say it was my fault, that he needed to take a break from me as I was too controlling. I didn't understand this. Dave could be aggressive. He would hit me, hard. He would pull me out of bed in the middle of the night by my hair to cook for him because he had either spent all day drinking and didn't want to eat, or he had spent all day in bed hungover from drinking too much the night before. I would have to make whatever he wanted and this ranged from toast with boiled egg to full meals such as lasagne from scratch and twice a full roast dinner. If I didn't make the dinner quickly enough or exactly how he wanted it, he would scream at me.

'What the fuck are you doing? You're fucking useless! Why the fuck do I keep you around? I could find someone better than you on a fucking street corner'.

I would think 'if I could just do better then he wouldn't shout at me, he would be happy and everything would be fine'. Looking back, I know I could have been Mother Theresa and I still wouldn't have been good enough for him because the problem wasn't with me, it was with him.

We would have sex anytime he wanted. It didn't matter where we were, how I was feeling or if I even wanted to at the time. On the days I were feeling ill or tired or just didn't want to, I would try to laugh it off and gently push him away.

'Babe I don't really feel well, why don't we just wait until tomorrow and I promise it will be better'. He never waited until tomorrow. He always got his way. In the beginning I would try to push him off, tell him I didn't want to, tell him to stop but I soon realised it was easier to let him do whatever he wanted as it would be over quicker.

The relationship was not always bad. When he was in a good mood he would treat me well. He would buy me flowers, clothes, jewellery, perfume, take me for lunch or dinner or away for the weekend. I felt like the good days outweighed the bad and even though it was a toxic relationship, I always felt safe with him. Yes, he would hit me and we had sex anytime he wanted, but whenever we were out together and I happened to see Alex or his friends, they would leave me alone. I was always grateful for this.

I was regularly sick all the time. I put it down to not eating enough and drinking too much or working too much so when I started being sick every day I never thought anything of it. At work I would have between five to nine cups of coffee per day, depending on how long my shift was. I was sitting at my desk one afternoon after making myself a coffee, it was one of those sachets that had coffee, sugar, and powered milk all in the one. When I began drinking it, I noticed it tasted like metal. I thought my sachets were out of date, even though the sell by date wasn't until the following year so I binned the coffee and went to the canteen to get a proper cup from the machine, however, this tasted the same. The girl sitting opposite me asked what was wrong and I told her I thought my tastebuds had finally had enough and were rejecting my coffee addiction as it all tasted like metal.

She laughed, looked right at me, and said, 'You're pregnant'. I laughed too as this thought was so ludicrous to me.

'No, I'm not. I replied.

'Yes you are' she said again and continued to laugh. Unbeknown to me, on her lunch break and while in a pharmacy, she picked up a pregnancy test. She text asking me to meet her in the bathroom. I initially thought something was wrong and immediately ran to the bathroom but when I got there, she held up the test and said, 'go pee on this'. I was convinced she was wrong so I did as she asked.

We stood chatting afterwards while the timer on her phone counted down the two minutes for the results. 'Times up' she said. 'Are you looking or am I'? she asked.

'You look, I already know the answer' I said confidently. She looked at me and again laughed.

'Congratulations'

I looked at the test and saw the black writing on the LED screen 'positive'. The room started spinning, I couldn't take my eyes off the result. Positive? How could it be positive? Then the fear and panic started to set in. I knew Dave would not be happy. I knew the relationship was not healthy. How could I bring a child into this? My colleague saw the panic on my face.

'It's okay. Everything is going to be okay. Just breathe' she tried to comfort me. She hugged me tight and walked me back to my desk. I was scared to tell Dave. I wasn't sure if I wanted to tell him just now or if I should wait until I had seen a doctor. I decided I had to tell him. He would regularly hit out at me and I couldn't take the chance he would hit me and harm the pregnancy. I text Dave to tell him I was not doing overtime and would be finishing at 5pm.

I got a taxi home as I couldn't face the bus journey and the anticipation of Dave's reaction was making me very anxious. I needed to tell him before I changed my mind and I had to prepare myself for whatever would come next.

I got out the taxi and had to stand for a few minutes until the shaking in my legs had ceased. I felt terrified. I had no idea how he would react. Would he be angry and hit me? Would he be excited and hug me? I couldn't take a second to think of how I was feeling as I was only thinking of Josh and his reaction. I made my way up the stairs to his door and I walked in. I could smell that he made dinner as I quietly closed the door and had already decided I would tell him as soon as I saw him.

I walked into the kitchen and saw Josh taking two plates out of the cupboard. He had made pasta bolognese, one of my favourites, and was starting to plate it up. He took a garlic bread baguette from the oven and I watched as he cut it with a large knife, put the knife into the sink and collected a beer from the fridge. He didn't turn around, didn't look at me. He just spoke.

'I've made dinner but there's football on so you'll have to do the dishes' he told me.

I stood there and counted down in my head....3.....2.....1.....

'I'm pregnant'. For a few minutes it felt like the world fell silent. He stood there, his back to me, not moving, not saying a word. I wondered if he had heard me. I didn't have to wonder much longer. Before I could comprehend what was happening, he lifted one of the plates in front of him, swung around and threw it at my head. I ducked and the plate, full of food, hit the doorframe and shattered. The walls, the door, the floor, and me were covered in pasta bolognese. As I stood there looking at the mess I thought how such a small plate of dinner could make so much mess.

I stood up, his face so close mine, and without saying a word I picked up my handbag and walked out. To this day I have never seen him again. Four days later I miscarried. I went to hospital on my own and told no-one. When I returned to work I told my colleague the test must have shown a false positive and I put it all to the back of my mind.

The second time I found out I was pregnant; I had already ended things with the guy I was seeing. His name was Luke and he was nice. We got along well, he made me laugh, we liked the same things and we did try but there was no spark.

Luke was smart, funny, tall with dark hair and hazel eyes. When he smiled, it was only ever with one side of his mouth. Luke was a gentleman. He would hold doors open for me, pull out chairs, ask me where I wanted to go and what I wanted to do. He would always try and pay for everything but I would insist everything be 50/50.

We remained friends for a short period after we broke up and it was during this time that I found out I was pregnant. I had decided to wait until I had seen a doctor before telling him as it was such a shock to me and because of my previous miscarriage. I called the doctor and got an appointment for six days later, however, before I could attend, I miscarried. I thought it was a punishment because I had finally found a decent guy who made me laugh instead of cry and I still couldn't commit. I got through it with the help of my friends and I moved on.

After my second loss, I was referred to a gynaecologist for tests. I was sceptical of any outcome and hadn't thought about seeing someone but my GP had referred me. I had a few tests done; bloods, internals, biopsies, scans and then I received a letter for an appointment regarding my results. I went along to the hospital on my own, sat in the red plastic chair and waited on my name being called. I entered the office and took a seat across from the doctor. She was tiny, had short black hair and olive skin. She was wearing a white doctor's jacket which made me chuckle as I had only ever seen people wear these on TV.

'I have your results. You have uterine scarring, commonly known as 'Asherman's Syndrome' she informed me. 'It's scarring, which is usually a result from surgery, however, you've never had surgery' she went on. She explained scarring can be a result of different things, one being trauma.

I sat there and didn't particularly have any strong feelings about what I was being told. I had two miscarriages, tests were done, the problem was found and it wasn't life threatening. It could be treated with surgery or heal on its own. I got up, thanked her, and left.

As I was leaving the hospital a thought suddenly hit me like a ton of bricks. 'Trauma to the abdomen' she had said. I had been in a few minor car accidents but none that resulted in hospital stays, but I had had repeated trauma to that area. As I slowly began to realise what she had said, how trauma had caused the miscarriages, how they, how he, had repeatedly kicked me, punched me, threw me against walls and car bonnets, I suddenly dropped to my knees. I sat on the floor in the middle of the main entrance to the hospital, and I sobbed. I thought taking my virginity was the worst thing he could have done, until now.

Chapter Sixteen

After that night, when I had thrown myself at boys, at men, I think I was trying to make myself believe I was okay, that what happened had not affected me. I didn't realise how dangerous my actions were. Then again maybe I did but didn't care.

I thought if I could kiss them, have them kiss me, have them touch me, let them have sex with me, then surely I was fine? I didn't dare get too close to any of them. I felt nothing for these people, I was hollow and no-one could offer me enough of anything to fill that hole inside me.

I have never been in love. As I got older, I thought it was all a lie. I thought that love was a word people threw around like confetti but didn't really hold any real meaning. People used it all the time. 'Oh, I love him, I love my dog, I love my job, I loved our holiday, I love summer, I love the cold, I love this boy band or TV show'. To me, love was a word I heard everyday but that was said so many times it had lost whatever meaning it was supposed to hold.

I was fourteen years old the night my life permanently changed. I had no experience with boys or love or sex. I was young and naïve. I was a child. I had no life experience. I had barely any experience about anything in this big bad world.

I did wonder about love, and lust. A part of me thought it was all a lie, the other part wanted to see if it were true. I had had many guys in my life and felt nothing. I was closed off with them, numb. I thought I could never love a male; I didn't feel anything towards them, not even hate. But I had always been comfortable around females. So, I went online and created an account on an online dating website.

Name: That was easy.

Age: Should I say I was older or younger? I decided to be me.

Location: Don't give a stranger your address. I put the name of the city I lived in. It was a big city.

Are you looking for males or females: I hadn't had any luck with males, I felt nothing towards them. I rarely felt safe but I did feel safer around people of the same sex. I clicked female.

As I was filling in the profile, I wondered if what Alex had done had caused me to possibly be attracted to the opposite sex or if it were something that would have happened anyway.

I finished setting up my profile, answering the usual questions: my hobbies, what music I liked, what my characteristics were, what I was looking for in someone, adding a photo, then it was live.

I started to browse the people who were online. Within a few minutes I got a notification, someone had liked my profile! 'Wow that was quick, they must have clicked on the wrong page' I thought. I opened her page and smiled as I saw her photo. Her name was Charlie; she lived over three hundred miles away and had two children who she shared custody of with her ex.

Charlie made me laugh; she was incredibly funny. We exchanged numbers and began to talk. She would ask about my day and I hers, she seemed interested in my responses too. We talked about my work, my friends, my family. I asked about her life, her interests, her hopes, and dreams for the future.

She asked me the same and it was only at that point I realised I didn't have any hopes or dreams for my future. I had always assumed I would die young and didn't bother planning for a life I thought I would never live.

I felt safe with Charlie. Maybe it was because she were so far away, a stranger, a voice at the end of the line. I began letting down my walls ever so slightly and slowly told her about my demons.

Charlie listened as I spoke. The longer her silence lasted, the more I divulged. I kept talking until I had nothing left to say, then I held my breath and waited. I was sure she had hung up by this point, rightly thinking I were some crazy person she needed to run from, but I was wrong.

'You are one of the strongest people I know' came her response. 'Thank you for sharing your story, and I hope you didn't do this to scare me away because it has made me want to hold onto you even tighter'.

A tear slid down my cheek as I finally let the air escape my lungs. After all this time I had finally told someone what had happened, and she didn't blame me, she didn't question it, she didn't run. She sat there and listened and for the first time in my life my heart fluttered.

The next day, at Charlie's insistence, I bought a train ticket to her town. I had to wait three days until I finished work and could go meet her and those were the longest three days of my life.

I told everyone I was going away for the weekend with different people. I told family I was going with friends, I told friends I was going with family, I told my work colleagues I were going with different friends as they already knew some of them.

I carefully packed my bag the night before. I was just the right amount of nervous and scared. I couldn't believe I were doing this. What if she didn't show? I hadn't booked anywhere to stay as she told me I would be staying with her. What if she didn't turn up? What if she saw me and left? I pulled out my phone to check how long I would be stranded at the train station for before I could get a return train home but a voice in my head made me stop. I was being ridiculous. If, when I got there, things weren't as great as we had planned, all I had to do was get on a train and come home. That wasn't difficult. I had to trust things would work out and have a little faith it would all be okay.

The next morning, I woke early and showered. I hadn't chosen an outfit the night before as I had no idea what to wear. Did I dress comfortably for the long train ride or dress-up for when I saw Charlie? I decided on something in between and chose a new pair of dark blue jeans, a light pink wrap around top and a pair of ankle boots. I looked at myself in the mirror. 'This is as good as it's going to get' I told myself.

I was nervous, my hands were shaking as I dialled the taxi number then waited outside. It was a 10-minute ride to the station and as the driver asked me where I were off too, I replied 'to see a friend'. It wasn't a lie but not quite the truth either. She was a friend, but she meant more to me than that. As I took a seat on the train facing forwards, my breathing slowed and my hands stopped shaking. I spent the next few hours looking out of the window and feeling excited at what was to come.

At 6pm the train slowly pulled into the station and my stomach was filled with butterflies. I lifted my handbag and my overnight bag before slowly stepped off onto the platform. I lifted my head to scan the crowd and heard a familiar voice.

'Lux'!

I turned around and there she was. Her brown hair shining and smooth as it cascaded around her shoulders, her piercing blue eyes locked on mine. She looked so good standing there waving at me with the biggest smile I had ever seen. She were wearing tight blue jeans with a white floral top and was holding a huge bunch of yellow flowers, my favourite, in her other hand. She walked towards me, my feet frozen to the spot, and threw her arms around my neck. I hated people touching my neck, but her arms felt soft and safe.

She smelled alluring, so subtly sweet, a mixture of perfume and flowers. It was intoxicating. Her smile travelled from her lips to her eyes and I stood there thinking how she surely would be appalled with me and send me on the next train home.

She didn't. She took my hand in hers and we walked to the carpark. She placed my bags into the boot then drove us to her home. It was a short drive and we talked like we had known each other our whole lives. It was so easy being with her. She had made us dinner, creamy chicken roulade with spinach and button mushrooms. It was delicious.

Afterwards we had some wine and sat on the couch talking until 4am. She was incredibly easy to be around. As I sat beside her, listening to her talk about her children, her work, her life, I suddenly realised I had never had this feeling with anyone else in my life. It terrified me. And it excited me. She seemed so interested in me; the places I had visited, the companies I had worked for, my childhood and my family. She knew what had happened to me but she never mentioned it, instead getting me to look at the positive things in my life. Something I rarely did.

Things with Charlie lasted only a year but we had some great times that I will forever cherish. In the end, the distance was just too much. We remained friends and periodically keep in contact. I will forever be grateful to her for the year we spent together and for her ease at which she allowed me to open up my heart.

A few years later, I was sitting one night at 1am still struggling with my sexuality and decided I needed to do something, I needed to know once and for all if I were supposed to be with a female, a male or if I were bi-sexual.

I went online, made a profile, and started looking around. Within minutes I came across this girl. Her smile was the first thing to catch my eye. As I read her profile I saw that she was smart and funny so I clicked the like button. She sent me a message a few minutes later and we spoke for hours.

The next day she asked for my number and I hesitantly gave it to her. That night as I was walking home from work, she called me. We were on the phone for 6 straight hours and when the call ended I felt like I could have easily spoken with her for another 6 hours.

We spoke every single day, multiple times a day. Our calls lasted between 3 and 6 hours each time. I once counted how long we had spent talking with each other on the phone and it was 14 hours. In one day!

We chatted about anything and everything. She shared her life with me and I shared my life with her. She also didn't live close but she was only an hour's train ride away.

Yes, things with Charlie had been amazing and I continue to be grateful to her but Chelsea had lit a different kind of fire inside me. I had never in my life felt this way about someone. When we weren't spending hours on the phone I spent hours thinking about her. We would video chat and often fell asleep on the phone to each other.

I was afraid of what my friends and family would think of my sexuality. Only one friend had known about Charlie but most of my friends knew about Chelsea. They were very supportive and only ever wanted the best for me. I did not share any of this with my family.

Things with Chelsea eventually fizzled out. Nothing had really caused this; it was all hot and heavy very quickly and was great while it lasted.

After Chelsea I dated some nice guys. Others not so nice. I wasn't as closed off in relationships as I once had been but I didn't unlock the chains around my heart. Even though I remained quite laid back when it came to decision making, I did put more of an effort into planning what we did or where we went. I was no longer afraid to have an opinion.

Chapter Seventeen

Everything with his friends calmed down and I had a good two-year break. I still lived my life on high alert, afraid of getting close to anyone, of being on my own. I still couldn't sit still, always needing to be kept busy, always had music on because I hated the sound of silence. I kept my guard and walls up because I knew this could change at any moment.

I would get taxis everywhere I went. If I got a text from a new number, for a moment my heart froze. I couldn't sleep unless there was music or the TV playing. On the rare occasions I was out alone, I had my earphones in and my music blaring. Something people say you shouldn't do while out on your own but it was better than jumping at every noise I heard. I'm still the same to this day. Memories would often flood my thoughts, agonizing memories that were like re-reading an old book that was ghastly so I carefully placed them upon a shelf and left them there to rot.

A few years ago, in autumn, the messages and calls started again. I did what I always do and ignored them. However, they were consistent. The messages and calls never mentioned the senders name but from reading and listening to these, I realised it was Dennis, or 'Denny Boy' as Alex would regularly call him. Great timing, I was just beginning to run out of nightmares.

I wasn't surprised when it started again, but I was curious as to why, after such a long break. This was the longest I had gone with no contact from any of them but I didn't have to wait long to find out.

'My brother, my best mate in the world should be here celebrating his big 40th birthday and because of you he's six feet under' one of the calls said. 'His mam is having to organise and pay for a balloon release instead of throwing him a party', he went on. 'He should fucking be here, celebrating with his mates, having a wife and kids and fucking having a great life but because you're such a fucking selfish bitch he's dead! He's fucking dead because of you! Don't you dare come to the balloon release or I'll kill you in front of everyone and they would all help me cut you up into tiny pieces once they knew who you really were'.

I was still confused, how was any of this my fault? Had he wanted me to report Alex to the police? He could have spent years in prison for everything he did and he still wouldn't have had a good life, a wife, or kids.

And did he really think I would attend a balloon release for the man who had taken so much from me? It was ludicrous, almost laughable. The calls kept coming, each one unanswered by me, each one giving him the opportunity to leave another message.

'Ha-ha I know where you work bitch! Think you can hide from me? You'll be fucking sorry when I get my hands on you! Alex ain't got nothing on me! You'll be begging me to end you when I'm done! I can do worse things than kill you!

This sent me into a panic. I was continuing to work in care and had a responsibility to keep everyone safe. Was he just saying this to get a reaction out of me or did he really know where I worked? Alex had always found out in the past so this was not me over-thinking things. 'Do we really need to play this game again' I whispered to myself. I could feel a storm coming and I didn't know if I had the strength to survive it again.

For a moment I did think about running and telling someone in work everything that happened, but that thought quickly evaporated as I remembered all too well that day in the call centre when the police were called. Instead, I approached someone I trusted and told them about the recent messages and the threat of coming to my work. I didn't dare divulge too much. She listened, confirmed I were safe while at work and made me promise not to walk home alone.

If he did know where I worked, then he wouldn't come in. He couldn't get inside anyway unless he was there to visit someone. This calmed my nerves a little.

I'm not sure if it were because I had such a gap, or maybe because I did feel guilty Alex wouldn't be here to celebrate his birthday with his friends and family, but I couldn't switch my brain and feelings off as easily as I once could. Over the years I became an expert at switching off, not only with them but with different things in my life. Everyone always said I was the person needed around whenever there was an emergency as I remained calm and knew exactly how to respond.

In the past a message like this would not even have registered. It would be read, or said aloud to me, and it would never be thought of again. But this time, it felt different. If felt dangerous.

The month following the start of the calls and texts, my friend's daughter sadly passed away. It was incredibly heart-breaking for everyone who had known her. She had been sick her whole life, the doctors told her parents she would never make it out of hospital when she was born, but she had. She came home, she smiled, she laughed, she had so many people around her who loved her unconditionally. Still, her passing left a huge empty space in the hearts of everyone who had ever had the privilege of being part of her life.

Two days before the funeral, I received a text message. 'Didn't know you knew big Joe, see you at the kid's funeral' it read. I turned my phone off and placed it down. I did not have the strength or the will to deal with that right now.

The funeral was on a Saturday, and even though it was almost winter, the sun shone high in the sky. The service itself was beautiful; filled with colour, happy memories, and at points even laughter. Loved ones held hands and prayed, the church filled with graceful handwritten poems being read aloud and her favourite music playing. She had been an amazing child.

After the service, we went back to a hall in a local pub. There were sandwiches, cakes, biscuits, tea, and coffee. It's funny isn't it, how we think a cup of tea and a scone can make a funeral more bearable?

I saw Dennis and his band of brothers as I were leaving the church but I kept my eyes down and walked past. I never saw them again until a few hours later as people started to leave the pub. I had been sitting with friends and as they left my aunt and cousins called me to their table.

'How's your mum and dad enjoying their holiday'? My aunt asked me. They had left a few days before. My back was towards the bar but I could feel his stare piercing into me.

'They're having a great time' I softly whispered. Praying he wouldn't hear me.

'When they due back'? My cousin asked. I wanted to turn around and check if he were close enough to hear our conversation but I dared not look.

'Thursday' I replied, barely above a whisper. I hated being so close to him, to them. My veins felt as though ice ran through them and I was struggling to calm my thoughts. I looked at my phone but I hadn't received one call or text all day. 'What did this mean'? I thought to myself.

The next night I was out walking my dog Max. It was around 9:30pm and it was getting colder. I had my warm coat on, a hat and leather gloves. I couldn't stand the feeling of a scarf against my skin, it was a constant reminder of Alex's hands against my throat. How he would press and hold so tightly that I often gasped for breath.

We took the same walk we did each night. We had done this so many times I'm sure I could have walked it with my eyes closed. There was a bus stop that we passed, it was off the main road and hidden from sight, only passengers and bus drivers would have known it was there.

Max stopped, as he did each night, and sniffed every inch of that bus shelter. Surely he had smelled everything it had to offer by now? I was watching Max, wagging his tail and loving life as I heard screeching tires. I instantly thought there had been some sort of accident, probably due to black ice on the road, but I hadn't heard another car. The bright lights from the car lit up the bus stop and Max came running to my side. It was dark and the lights shining on me made it difficult to see. Then I heard his voice.

'Have fun ignoring me all day yesterday did you'? I heard as a punch caught me in the stomach and I fell to the ground. The car engine was turned off and the lights died. I was holding on tight to Max's lead but as Dennis pulled me to my feet I felt another pair of hands pull the lead from mine.

'No'! I screamed out and heard laughing. A blow to my chest made it difficult to breathe. I saw a man I didn't recognise take Max to the back of the car as Dennis, pulling me by my hair, opened the car door and pushed me inside. I was laying on my back in the backseat of the car. A spark of light made me look at the driver's seat and I saw someone sitting there. I couldn't see enough to know who it was, or even if I knew him. He lit a cigarette, turned the car engine on, keeping the lights off and turned on the music. All I could think of was Max and getting him back.

Dennis was still holding me by my hair, his face pushed up close against mine. I could feel the warmth of his skin against my cold cheek, I could see his lips moving but were struggling to understand what he was saying as everything sounded muffled.

I tried to fight. I managed to kick him in the leg and he jumped back, stepping outside the car. I pulled myself up using the headrest of the passenger seat and tried to get out. My only thought was Max and keeping him safe. I wasn't thinking of myself at all.

My jacket was unzipped as I hated being warm and never wore it fastened. He pulled me out of the car by my collar and threw me onto the ground.

'Where the fuck you think you're going'? He snapped as he spit in my face. He was on top of me again, his eyes so dark, like black holes piercing into me. His teeth were clenched as he punched at my stomach and chest.

'Please don't to this' I whispered.

'Say that again' he spat. 'I love it when you beg'.

I saw a flash of silver and my eyes locked on Alex's pocketknife. Alex loved that thing. I don't know what he loved more, having that on him 24/7 or when he used it to cut into my skin. It wasn't sharp, but sharp enough to make me bleed and leave my skin with scars.

Dennis was waving the knife around, holding it like a child trying to impress his friends but at the same time waving it around carelessly like it were a toy. I couldn't take my eyes off it, waiting and wondering where it would pierce me first.

'Woof' I turned my head to the side and saw Max. His tail was wagging and the man holding onto his lead was on his knees behind the car. He was shaking a set of keys that had what looked like a green fluffy toy attached to them. I remember thinking it looked more like something a girl would have on her keys. Max was jumping around trying to catch it, playing with this stranger, oblivious to what was happening around him. I knew he was going to be okay.

He did try to run over to me a couple of times but the stranger held him back by his lead and would shake his keys again, distracting Max from what was happening to me. He was laughing as Max jumped and spun around in circles, excited for this new game. It was surreal. I was scared to make any loud noises or sudden movements in case they took Max away or hurt him.

Dennis was breathless. He smelled of stale beer, like the way a pub smells at the end of the night when all the empty pint glasses are sitting on the bar waiting to be cleaned. It made me feel sick.

I tried to breathe through my mouth so I wouldn't smell it then he kissed me. He was enraged, hitting me repeatedly, but never in the face. Then I heard a familiar sound, the sound of him unzipping his jeans and I knew what was coming. He felt so heavy on top of me, I tried to move but I couldn't. He was using his knees to keep me from moving around, digging them hard into my legs and stomach. I could feel it, but I didn't feel any pain. I lay there wishing that someone would drive past and help me, hoping that no-one else would be out walking their dog in case they too got hurt. 'Do we really have to play this game again? I said to myself.

I was trying to push him off, hold him away but he used his elbows to swat at my hands. My hands, now in fists, tirelessly trying to hit him anywhere I could. But nothing stopped him. I didn't scream, I didn't make a sound. I didn't say no or stop or get off or get away. I was fighting, but I was silent. I would turn my head when he tried to kiss me, this caused him to bang my head off the ground. The hood of my jacket stopped it from being too serious, giving me some support so my head wouldn't bleed.

He started pulling at the neck of my t-shirt, trying to force his hands down my top. 'Why isn't he pulling my t-shirt up, doesn't he know how much easier that would be for him'? I asked myself. It appeared that he had very little idea of what he was doing. The back of my neck started to burn from him pulling at the front.

He started tugging at my jeans, trying to tear them off. He was becoming angrier, swatting my hands away, digging his knees into me with the full weight of his body. Grunting. He barely said a few sentences and stopped looking at me. He was becoming obsessed at getting what he came for. Became obsessed with having me. He had told me in his sea of messages that he would do exactly what Alex had done to me, and he was about to make good on his promise.

He finally managed to unzip my jeans then he stopped for a second, a look of uncertainty on his face. For a moment I though he were having second thoughts, that he would let me go. But he didn't. He pulled out his penis, crawled up until he was sitting on my chest and pinning my arms down then he tried to put it into my mouth. I clenched my jaw tightly shut and could feel it slapping against my face as I moved my head from side to side, trying to escape it.

'You fucking stupid bitch'! He screamed at me. 'Open your fucking mouth'. But I refused to. He slapped me in the face before finally stopping, moved backwards down my body and then he was inside me.

I kept my eyes on Max. 'Please don't let him see this' I thought to myself. It was a strange thought to have. He was a dog, what difference would it make if he saw me or not, he couldn't tell anyone. Max was still wagging his tail, still trying to catch the fluffy keyring, oblivious to what was going on around him. 'The next few moments will either glide swiftly by or they'll be the concluding injustice that permanently breaks me' I thought to myself.

It hurt. It really hurt. I lay there looking at the sky and wondering if it hurt more this time than when it had done that night with Alex but before I could fully compare the two, it was over. He was done. He sat there on top of me, still inside me, and laughed. How strange his laugh was, it sounded so normal. The laugh of someone having a good time and not of someone who had just raped me.

I tried to get up but his hand swiftly made its way to my neck, pushing me down. An all too familiar feeling. I lay there on the ground, my body limp, arms by my sides. I felt nothing. My head was silent, my body told me of no pain. I could hear no sounds. For a few seconds I wondered if I had died and not yet realised it.

He stood up, picking up the pocketknife he had dropped at some point and adjusted his clothing as he stared at me. If I were dead, would I remember this? Would his eyes be the last thing I ever saw? And if I had lived, what would happen next? What would my life look like now? When it happened before, my whole world changed. Could it get any worse?

'Are you going to kill me'? I asked him.

'Maybe, maybe not' he laughed. His eyes were bitter and desolate as he looked at me.

I closed my eyes and tried moving my fingers. Okay, I could feel them moving. I wiggled my toes; I could feel that too. I tried to lift my head a little off the ground, it started pounding, which was a good sign, it confirmed I was still alive. My arms felt heavy, but with my eyes still closed I gave it everything I had left, which was not much, and I attempted to push myself up.

'You don't fucking move until I say so, you hear me'? He had leaned down over me. 'Don't. Fucking. Move'. I could suddenly hear Max again as he panted from excitedly playing with his new friend. I turned my head to look at him then let out a scream as I felt a sharp pain in my left hand. It felt as though my bones had shattered. I looked across in time to see him lifting his foot from my hand as he continued to laugh. The pain was almost unbearable.

He took a few steps towards the car and the driver handed him a packet of cigarettes. He took these, pulled a lighter from his pocket and took a draw. He looked quite pleased with himself, like he was proud of what he had just accomplished. When he finished his cigarette he threw the butt onto my stomach. I grabbed it with my right hand and threw it away.

Dennis walked around to the passenger's side and got in. I could hear the footsteps of Max's new friend coming towards me. Max was suddenly at my face, licking me and barking, wanting me to play with him. The guy helped me to my feet, wiped some dirt from my jacket and waited until I had adjusted myself before handing Max back to me. The music was now blasting from the car, echoing all around.

'You hurt'? He half smiled at me before getting into the back of the car. 'Your hand is bleeding'.

'Oh really? I hadn't noticed the blood flowing from my veins but thanks for pointing that out' I thought to myself but said nothing.

It all felt surreal. Did this just happen? Had I imagined it? Surely if something like that had happened again, I would feel it? The world would feel it? Feel something? I looked at Max who was trying vigorously to get to the grass. I walked him over. I finished his walk, the usual route we took each night before we headed home.

I took his lead off as we entered the garden, something I always did and watched as he ran from one end to the other. I unlocked the door and stepped inside. I straightened my arms and my jacket slid off my shoulders as it fall onto the floor. I walked into my kitchen, my safe heaven. The spotlights cast an eerie glow as I stumbled across the floor to the sink, washed my hands before collapsing onto the cold tiles. I didn't make a sound. I didn't cry or wince in pain. I sat there on the cold tiles, my legs folder underneath me, my head resting against the cupboard door and stared at nothing. I didn't reach for the phone to call for help. I didn't attempt to get up and shower, I didn't take Max to bed as I usually did. I sat there emotionless and with an empty mind for hours.

When the sun came up I turned towards the window. My neck was stiff from being in the same position for so long. There was a glass vase on the windowsill and I watched as the sun's rays hit it and colours danced around the kitchen walls. It was a new day.

I looked down at my hand. It was the first time I had looked at it and instantly noticed how swollen it was. Bruising already making its appearance on the skin and it felt tight. I was struggling to make a fist.

I had training today. It felt like a distant memory but I knew it was today. I slowly stood, all my limbs still attached and working properly, and I walked into the living room. Max was sound asleep on the couch; I kissed his head and make my way upstairs. I picked out my clothes, lay them on the bed and walked into the bathroom.

I turned on the shower, took out everything I needed from the bathroom unit, collected a towel from the cupboard and started to undress. Every inch of my body ached; my muscles burned, my skin felt raw, even the hairs on my arms and legs felt broken. I looked in the mirror and saw a familiar sight as fresh red bruising started to appear on my skin. I knew how this went. At first the red bruising, after a day or two it would turn blue or purple, depending on how hard the blow to that particular area had been and then as it started to fade it would turn green and yellow.

I stood in the shower and let the water flow over me. My skin felt hot. It always did after a beating. To this day I dislike being warm as it reminds me of all those times I was hurt. I would rather be freezing cold than feel the heat. I turned the temperature on the shower down, lifted my sponge, poured shower gel onto it and started washing off the night before. I winced in pain as the soap entered cuts and grazes on my skin and let out sighs as my muscles cried from being used at all.

Once I was finished, I stepped out the shower, dried, dressed and tied my hair in a bun. The thought of the heat and the effort of using my hairdryer and straighteners was too much to bear at that moment.

I looked out my best make up and carefully applied this to my face. There was not much to hide, most of the injuries were on my torso, arms and legs which made me relax a little. 'No funny stares' I told myself as I looked in the mirror and admired how well I had hidden the bruising. I walked downstairs, said good morning to Max, put on his lead and we walked outside. We had the same daily walk; the same routing and I didn't question the way my feet were leading us. I was thinking of the training that day, it was only three hours and I didn't know anyone else who would be there. This didn't bother me as I would chat with anyone. Working in a pub had taught me a lot about small talk.

As I came out of my thoughts about training, I realised we were standing at the bus stop. The exact location where last night's events took place. I stood looking at the spot where I had lay, the spot Max had stood playing, the space the car had taken up the previous night. My body knew it had been no dream but my head was still trying to catch up to that.

Max pulled me, almost knowing it wasn't a good place to be and we continued his walk. When we returned home I made him breakfast, filled his water bowl, called a taxi, kissed him on the head and left for training.

Chapter Eighteen

It was bizarre. Inside I could feel it, I could feel I wasn't okay. I tried to stop and think, I wanted it to hit me, I needed it to hit me because it all felt too dreamlike to be true. I wanted to cry but was battling the two people inside me. One who wanted to get on with her day, get through training and go home so she could hide with her dog. The other, screaming inside me, feeling nothing but pain and torment, wanting so desperately to be let out just this once and tell the world how much she were hurting.

As usual I composed myself enough to walk into the building and find my way to the training room. It was filled with huge round tables that were slowly starting to fill with people but I didn't recognise anyone which made me relax. At least I didn't have to paint on a happy face for someone who already knew me and may see through it.

'There's an empty chair here if you need a seat' one woman smiled at me. She was older than I was, had bright fiery orange hair and red glasses. I thanked her and sat down. Everyone else at the table knew each other and began introducing themselves to me. They had once all worked together but some were now working elsewhere. The group were loud, not caring about who heard or seen them as everyone around us took their seat.

I smiled, laughed, and nodded on que. I listened to what the trainers were saying but none of it were making its way to my brain. I wasn't bothered much by this as the training was mandatory for my new job, however, I had spent a few years training it in my previous job.

We took a break half-way through. One of the women asked if I wanted a tea or coffee and I instantly attempted to stand but she told me to sit down.

'You're better doing what she says' another of the women at the table informed me. 'She's the mama bear. If you don't tell her whether you want tea or coffee, she'll bring you both' she laughed.

'Tea please' I smiled politely.

She brought back a tray filled with tea and coffee, milk, sugar sachets and biscuits. Lots of biscuits. As we sat around the table chatting and laughing, some filling me in on the others antics while the others proclaimed their innocence, I realised we were all women. I'm not sure why I noticed this but it helped me to relax even more.

'This is positively insane' I thought to myself. Here I am, sitting with all these women around me, at a training about protecting others from harm, and it physically hurts to breathe after what happened the night before. I wondered what would happen if I stood up right now and confessed to the assault. Would anything happen? Would they think I were clinically insane? Would they believe me? Would they help me? I didn't need their help. Would they contact my work and tell them what I said? Tell them I were unfit to continue in my role? I hoped not, I wanted this job to be different. I decided it better to keep my secret to myself and pretend everything was okay.

After training one of the women asked me where I was going and I told her. She asked if I drove and I said no. She explained she was going shopping in my town and could drop me off but this sent a chill down my spine. I know she was just being polite and friendly but I hated getting into cars with people. Even with people I knew well. Most of my cousins were older, a few drove and I could easily count on one hand the number of times I have been in cars with them driving, and I had known them my whole life! I hated being in people's cars as they were in charge, they were the drivers and could take you anywhere, do anything and you were stuck. I'm still the same to this day, no matter how much I know or trust the driver.

She sat staring at me as my mind teared through excuses but I couldn't think of a single one. I was in pain. I was tired. I wanted to be home so I looked up and told her that would be great. The drive was only twenty minutes long and she talked easily about her kids the whole time. When we got out the car I thanked her and walked to the taxi rank, my legs still shaking from the car ride. As I stood there, I knew what I had to do next.

I got home, changed into jeans and a t-shirt then took Max for a walk. We walked straight past the place it had happened the night before and as Max sniffed every inch of the bus stop for the second time that day, I stood looking at the ground where I had lay. I wasn't sad or angry. I wasn't scared or upset. I was determined. We finished the walk and headed home. I filled up Max's water bowl, left out a few treats, kissed his head as he lay on the couch and walked into the bathroom to splash cold water on my face. My hands gripped tightly to the small porcelain sink in the downstairs bathroom as I told myself I could do this, that I had to do this. I closed my eyes, counted to ten to steady myself then I left, locking the door behind me.

The air was fresh but not too cold. I had put a cosy long grey cardigan over my t-shirt before I left and it was enough to keep me feeling comfortable as I walked the forty-minutes to the nearest police station. I could easily have gotten a bus or taxi there but I needed to walk. I needed to feel like I, myself, had done this and not have someone else drive me there. It was a crazy reason but I needed to do this alone, on my terms.

I confidently walked into the station and headed straight to the reception desk. The girl behind the desk was small, had light blonde hair tied up in a ponytail and was stapling some files together as I approached. I could hear voices behind her but couldn't see anyone else.

'Hi, how can I help you'? She smiled.

'Hi, I was attacked last night but don't want to press charges. I'm wondering if there's anyone I can talk to about options I have'? I asked, my voice remaining strong. She took my name and asked me sit down. A few minutes later a male officer approached and asked me to follow him. He took me through a set of doors and into a small room. It was exactly like I thought a police room would look like. There was a metal desk sitting in the middle of the room with three small white chairs scattered around it. The walls had been blue at some point in time but now were greyer in colour. The door had a square frosted window at the top so no-one could see in and the door itself was covered in scratches and dents.

The officer was tall, had jet black hair, muscles that looked as though they would burst through his uniform at any second and his voice was low as he spoke.

'Are you here alone'? He asked.

'Yes' I replied.

'I understand there was some trouble last night'? He gently pressed. 'Can you tell me about that'? I sat there in silence. Not because I was regretting my decision or that I was scared in case they had been following me that day and saw where I was. I was silent as I wondered where to start. I must have sat there longer than I thought because the officer got up, left, and returned with a female officer. She smiled as she sat down placing a white plastic cup of water and a packet of tissues in front of me.

She looked about ten years older than me, had tired gentle eyes and when she spoke, it was barely above a whisper. Her auburn hair was pulled back in a loose bun and she placed her hand gently on mine. I looked into her eyes and started at the beginning. I told them about the night I first met Alex, what happened the next night, explained everything that happened over the years including his death and being at his funeral, right up to and including the night before. I pulled out my phone and showed them the calls and texts I had received, let them listen to the voicemails he had sent then stood up and showed them the marks on my body and my swollen hand.

They sat in silence as the male officer wrote everything down. I explained I didn't want to press charges but that I couldn't do this anymore. My left hand was on my lap and my right hand was on the table. As I looked down I saw the table was wet. I lifted the cup of water to see if it had been leaking but I couldn't find anything, then I realised I were crying. It was the strangest feeling as I hadn't noticed and thought how ridiculous I must have looked.

The female officer put her hand on my back and told me how brave I was. I rolled my eyes and laughed. Why did everyone tell me I was brave? What the hell did they know? I wasn't brave. If I had been, I would have come to the police long before now and I hadn't. I would have spoken to someone, anyone but I remained silent.

I gave them my phone and the male officer left the room. He returned later and told me he had taken note of the messages and call log, taken Dennis's phone number and asked me if I knew where he lived. I didn't but I opened Diane's Facebook and showed them a photo of him along with his profile.

The officers tried rationalising with me, telling me I had come this far and they would support me in pressing charges but I explained I couldn't and eventually they understood this.

They informed me how the laws around stalking and harassment had changed and there was more they could do now. They went on to say they would attempt to locate him and have a chat, related the information I had given today would be recorded and held on record for six months but would not show up on a police check unless charges were filed.

'If you change your mind within the next six months, you can come to us and we'll pick up from where we end today. If it's over the six months, we'll need to start from the beginning'. I thanked them for listening and telling me my options then I left.

A few days later I was sitting watching TV when my phone rang. It was the male officer calling to inform me they had located Dennis and spoken with him. He had been made aware I contacted the police and given information regarding his recent actions. The officer thought they had been firm enough with him that he should back off. He again asked if I wanted to press charges and I said no. I thanked him for all his help and hung up.

As soon as the call ended I called Tink. She was at work but could answer her phone. I was crying so heavily I couldn't get my words out and had to hang up. She immediately called back but I couldn't answer. I did manage to send a text telling her everything that had happened in the last few days, everything but how far he had gone. I apologised for not calling her or Lexi sooner, told her I were fine and would call back after she finished work.

Tink replied saying how proud she was of me, that I was brave and she was there any time I needed anything. I thanked her and put down my phone. I walked Max before giving him his dinner then we both crawled into bed. I lay there petrified, wondering if I would see Dennis again, and if I did, what would happen next.

Chapter Nineteen

After that Sunday night, and before the police called me back, I was in work. I had continued to work in care and we were required to wear medical gloves when assisting someone. I usually wore a medium size but my hand was so swollen it wouldn't fit. I tried a large and that was the same. I tried an extra-large and that wouldn't fit either.

I had seen a few colleagues giving me sideward glances over the previous few days but I ignored it. Some asked what happened and were told I had fallen when walking Max. I shrugged them all off and smiled as I had only recently started this job and didn't want anyone to think I were some kind of freak.

The temperature in work was particularly warm and I was becoming increasing annoyed at having to wear long sleeves in order to keep the marks on my body covered. My hand throbbed every second of the day and I felt drained. I was done having to hide, I was done pretending I was okay and nothing was wrong, I was done feeling the burning sensations running through my body and the pain was becoming excruciating.

There had been four or five colleagues that morning who asked if I were okay. I know they were concerned but I was tired and annoyed at everyone's constant questioning. I heard some of them mention approaching the person in charge that day about concerns they had for me. This made me panic.

What would she do? What would she say? Would she even speak to me about it? I felt I had to get in front of this to gain control so I went and knocked on her door. Gayle was sitting behind the desk.

'Do you have a minute' I asked

'Yes' replied Gayle.

'Has anyone said anything to you about me today'? I enquired.

'No' responded Gayle with a puzzled look on her face.

I briefly informed Gayle that something had happened, my hand was too swollen to wear a glove and people were talking about me. She asked to see my hand and I showed it to her. She advised I get it checked out at the hospital but I couldn't do that. Around the fifth or sixth time I went to hospital with a broken bone, the doctor told me if it happened again they would have to investigate what was happening. This terrified me and I only ever returned to hospital or went to my GP if it was absolutely necessary.

Gayle asked if I had further injuries and I nodded. I told her I had bruising over my whole body and I placed my hand on the cuff of my cardigan to show her the marks further up my arm, but I stopped. I hung my head and felt too ashamed to show her anymore.

As she questioned me about what happened, I could barely speak. The voice in my head was screaming at me to speak up, to tell her, to trust her with not only what happened a few days ago but with everything that happened since that cold February night when I was 14 years old. Gayle sat quietly and listened to the little I did say. She appeared very calm, still. She wasn't firing questions at me or telling me what to do, she was controlled and for the first time in days I felt as though I could relax as I took a deep breath. She told me if I couldn't talk about everything, to try going home and writing it down. I wasn't very good at putting my thoughts and feelings down onto paper and the last time I did, it hadn't ended so well. She went on to tell me I didn't need to answer any questions from my colleagues, to take a minute off the floor if I needed too and she reminded me I could talk with her anytime. She finished by advising me to change my phone number. I left the office and returned to work as thought nothing had happened.

I started to open up little by little to Gayle. She was easy to talk to. One day I was in the office talking with her about work when she asked me to sit down and I did. She proceeded to tell me she was extremely concerned about me, that she had a duty of care to me, had seeked advice from someone else and was waiting to hear back from them. I was shocked. She told me I could trust her and I had. I should never have trusted her though as here she was telling me she had seeked advice from someone else. I knew I had said too much, I had shared too much with her and all I wanted was to take it all back. I hated letting people in, I always ended up regretting it one way or another.

She wouldn't tell me who she had spoken with, what she had relayed to them or how long I had to wait to find out what they said. I was scared. I was tired. And I felt let down, again. Gayle never did tell me who she had spoken with but I learned months later it was with my manager.

A few days later I did attend hospital to have my hand checked. I had broken enough bones in my life to know it was not okay. I told the nurse I had gotten it trapped in work and she sent me for an x-ray. The results concluded I had broken bones in two of my fingers and broken my knuckle. She gave me painkillers, strapped my fingers together and sent me home. I was off work for the next few days and I kept the strapping on, however, the night before I was returning to work I removed it. People were already asking too many questions; I did not need them asking more.

That December I was in work plating dinner when a member of staff named Holly appeared with a beautiful bunch of flowers. I made a joke about how she didn't need to buy me flowers, she laughed and said they were for me. I thought she were only playing along but when everyone asked who the flowers were for she told them me. I froze. My feet unable to move. The plate of soup in my hands burning my fingertips but I couldn't move.

My colleague Heather took the bowl from my hands and told Holly to leave the flowers in the office. We followed behind and I managed to find my voice.

'Just leave them on the desk, I'll look at them after dinner is done' I pleaded.

'They're beautiful, who are they from'? Holly asked.

'Oh, I don't know, I'll look later when we've finished serving up dinner' I replied.

'Is there a card? There's a card! Open it! See who they're from' Heather excitedly told me.

My hands shaking, I carefully took the card from the centre of the bouquet and opened it. 'Merry Crimbo, D xx' was written inside. The flowers had a sticker on the outside saying 'Princess Bouquet'. I felt sick. I couldn't think. The room was spinning and I started to cry. Holly took me to a quiet room until I had calmed down.

The person in charge came into the room and immediately started to apologise for bringing the flowers round without first checking with me. I told her not to be silly. Receiving flowers was supposed to be a nice thing and why would they ever think that it wasn't? I didn't tell them anything about who had sent them and when I was calm enough I returned to work. I asked Heather to do something with the flowers, anything with them, take them home, share them between the residents, give them to another member of staff. I left that night without them and when I returned in the morning I was told a staff member had taken them home. I was so relieved. Two days later I received a text message calling me a selfish bitch and telling me I would be sorry for not thanking him.

Gayle had previously suggested I change my number. After being to the police and handing over all the information I had, I felt this was now something I was ready to do. I had held the same mobile number for six years over my last three phones and was unsure if or how I could have this changed.

I retrieved my laptop, signed into my mobile providers account, and opened a live chat. I informed the woman on the other line I was looking to have my number changed.

'Why'? She asked.

Why? I thought to myself. I hadn't anticipated this question, how foolish of me. Of course, they were going to ask why. As I sat there staring aimlessly at the blinking cursor, different scenarios ran through my mind. Did I tell her what he did to me a few nights ago? No, this was an innocent person at the end of this chat just casually going about her day, she did not need that horror in her head. How about telling her I worked for MI5 and it was top secret, which would be a story she could tell.

'Because the police advised me to' I explained. She didn't ask for any further explanation. She communicated that a signal would be sent to my phone within a few minutes, all I had to do was wait, turn my phone off and on again and my number would be changed. It was that easy. She continued to explain that for a few days both of my numbers would be live meaning if someone called or text my old number I would receive it and if I replied, it would be sent from my new number. She further went on to explain there would be no charge for this, however, if I needed it done again then I would incur a charge.

During those few days between having two numbers live, I continued to receive calls and texts from Dennis so I blocked his number, just as I had done so many times in the past with him and with Alex. I finished my eight-hour shift one day and took my phone out my handbag to find 127 blocked calls from his number. 127 calls between 9:07 and 14:35! Obviously he knew his number had been blocked so why keep trying?

So, my number was changed. I thought I would feel better but I didn't. I didn't like being alone in the carpark at work in case he was standing there watching me, waiting for me. I put my headphones in and blasted music as loud as I could from bands such as Skillet, Disturbed, Rise Against and Three Days Grace. The louder, angrier the music, the more relaxed I felt. If I were walking Max, I would keep my eyes on the ground directly in front of me in case he drove past.

I was either working or at home. I stopped going out. I did all my shopping online or asked my dad to pick things up and I only ever answered the door if I knew for sure who was standing on the other side. Six days later I received a text. It read 'Miss me'? I sat down on my kitchen floor, an empty shell of myself. Every bit of hope evaporated from my pores. My eyes welled up; I felt my throat closing as tears began to stream down my face. Without a single finger being placed on me this time, I felt beaten.

His texts went on to school me in Prepaid phones. I was told a sim card cost only 99p and I could block him as many times as I wanted to, but he wasn't going anywhere. I felt defeated. Deflated. Broken.

After this revelation, I stopped blocking his number, it was pointless and he acted as though he enjoyed this challenging game of cat and mouse. And the messages were all the same anyway no matter what number he text me from. He would tell me Alex was dead because of me, he would do worse to me than Alex did, I couldn't hide because he would always find me; telling me to kill myself because no-one liked me anyway and there was no-one who would miss me. He told me he had 'good drugs' which I could use to end my life, tell me all it would take is two little slits to my wrists and it would all be over. I could tell by the tone of his texts he was becoming angrier. This should have scared me, however, by this point I was living my life on autopilot and nothing - good or bad, could penetrate deep enough for me to care about. I had switched off from all reality.

On 6th April 2020, Dennis was texting his routine drivel and I was busy omitting his existence. I went to bed around 2am and checked his last few messages. I quickly noticed I hadn't received anything in a few hours which was surprisingly uncommon for him and heightened my inquisitiveness. I warily scanned his last messages.

His last array of messages were sent at 00:01 on 7th April and declared 'mibi al just dae masel in & blame u, thn ye wid huv don 2 eh iz in, wit ye evn dain ignorn me ya cunt, no scard eh me naw u shud b, al fkn huv the last laugh. This translates to: maybe I will do myself in and blame you, then you would have done 2 of us in, what you even doing ignoring me you cunt, not scared of me no you should be, I'll fucking have the last laugh.

Six hours later, at 8am I received an erratic call from my cousin Diane who informed me that Dennis was found unconscious early that morning on the floor by his brother, he had taken an overdose. She called back the following day to notify me of his death. She was overcome with emotion and I tried my best to calm her.

I am aware I didn't buy the drugs, or force open his mouth and pour them down his throat, but I felt astonishingly responsible for what he had done. I have since read and re-read those last few text messages hundreds of times. Had I not seen it? Were the messages the same or different to his usual ones? Had I inwardly known what he was going to do and selfishly did nothing as it would aid me in being free? Could I have done something? Done anything to stop him?

I hated Dennis but not as much as I had hated Alex. That word hate, it's definition 'feel intense dislike for' was not powerful enough for the way I felt about Alex. But I still would never have wished him dead. Not Dennis. I guess I would have to find a way to conquer this guilt just as I had done before.

He had told me in previous messages that he 'didn't care what the bhoys said, he would never forgive me for killing Alex' and with his passing now too, I slowly began to wonder if it was over. Could I finally get my life back? Did I have to be scared all the time? Did I have to spent every day looking over my shoulder or hiding from my phone? Was it done? Was I finally free? Turned out fate had one more card up his sleeve. And what a card it was.

Chapter Twenty

I was at work on 21st April 2020 and had a pounding headache so went to my locker for painkillers. I live with some form of headache every day and have done since I was young so I'm pretty good at knowing what caused it and which cocktail of drugs to mix to ease it quickly. Today's headache had been caused by lack of fluids, two hours sleep and continuous complaining from people around me so I took two aspirin, two ibuprofen and drank a full bottle of water. It didn't take the headache away but it calmed it enough I could make it through my shift before I started throwing up.

Before I placed my bag into my locker, I thought I would have a quick look and see if I had any messages. As I looked down at my phone I saw a familiar number, it was a text from Dennis's phone. It read: so ur the slut tht killd big Al & Denny. Nxt funeral is urs.

It seemed for a moment that time stood time. I couldn't think, I couldn't hear, I couldn't move, not even sure if I were breathing or holding my breath. Another member of staff came into the staff room and slowly brought me back to reality.

I reminded myself I was at work and Dennis was dead. It was just some sick joke and I still had four hours left of my shift. I turned the phone off, placed it back into my locker and went back to work like nothing had happened. On the outside I was fine, I smiled and laughed with the people I cared for, I listened and responded appropriately to other staff and I made sure all my duties were fully carried out before I finished my shift.

Over the next few days, I received more texts from a different number, all saying some version of that first one. It was funny, through all the texts and calls over the years, and there easily had been thousands, I never once replied or answered a call. And I had no plan of breaking my streak now so I blocked that number too. When the messages came from a different number, I gave up. Just like Dennis, the invisible texter was clearly getting off on me blocking them so why bother?

✳ ✳ ✳

My sister called me around 6:30pm one night to tell me my nephew had a throat infection; a high temperature and they had no medicine. This was a few months into a global pandemic where people were not permitted to leave their homes unless it was for work or emergency reasons. You had to stay close to home and if found farther away, you would be questioned by police if they saw you. But my nephew was sick and I had the medicine he needed so I broke the rules.

I decided against taking Max with me as he might draw attention which I did not need. I worked in care and had a letter confirming this which I could use should I be stopped on the way to or from work so I looked this out and I headed off.

The walk was not long. When I got there I opened the front gate, placed the medicine bottle at her front door and waved to my sister and nephew through the window. I stepped back, closed the garden gate, and continued until I was standing in the middle of the carpark, a good safe distance from everyone. My sister opened her front door, picked up the medicine, shouted 'thank you', waved at me and closed the door. It was a heart-wrenching time.

I put my headphones in and commenced the walk home. I had not passed anyone on the way to my sisters and I was feeling confident, cocky even that I would not be seen on the way home so I started to relax, just a little.

I had made this walk many times in the past and felt confident I could complete it with my eyes closed, however, I decided against that as knowing my luck I would have walked into a lamppost or a tree or a bus shelter. I wouldn't, however, have walked into a single person or any vehicles as there were none around.

I was half-way home and walking through a tunnel. It was small and stretched from one side of the road to the other. I could have crossed the deserted road and still would have come to the end of tunnel but as I was trying to stay out of view, I took the tunnel.

There was a guy walking through towards me. He was dressed all in black, but so was I so I didn't think much of this. He smiled at me and I could see his lips moving but my music was too loud to hear what he were saying so I removed my headphones.

'Got a light'? He asked. I could see an unlit cigarette in his left hand.

'Sorry I don't smoke' I smiled back.

'No bother' he said as he passed me.

I put my headphones back in and took a few steps before I felt an accelerated jolt to the back of my head then a strength throwing me against the wall of the tunnel. My arms stretched, trying to catch my balance; my stomach did a flip and I had a sickening sense that my knees would not support me. I felt a sharp yank as my head was snapped backwards by someone pulling on my hair.

'It has to be the guy who asked for a lighter' I told myself. 'There was no-one else around'. I tried to remember what he looked like, what he sounded like, what he was wearing. His face had been a shadow, my eyes only caught his smile as he opened his mouth to speak and the light bounced from his teeth. He sounded normal, no accept, no deep or high-pitched voice and he was dressed in all black. 'You should have being paying better attention', I scolded myself.

He just held me there for a few seconds. Breathing heavily in my left ear but not saying a word. I couldn't smell him, there was no bad aftershave, no signs of cigarette smoke and his breath felt sharp against my cheek as though he had just been eating a mint. My face was scratching against the dark damp wall of the dimly lit tunnel. I could feel those little pieces of sand like cement breaking from the sandpaper effect my face was having against the tunnel wall and felt them burrowing themselves into my skin. Then he harshly kicked at my legs and I dropped rapidly to the ground.

Everything happened in slow motion after this. From the corner of my eye, I saw a flash of silver and instinctively pulled my arms up to my head to try and protect my face. It had been a warm day with a few strong summer showers and I was wearing a black vest top with a thin black cardigan which had ¾ sleeves. I felt sharp scratches to my arms and hands as the small knife glided through my skin and just like that, as quickly as it started, it stopped. He grabbed me by the back of my neck, standing behind me and shielding his identify while spitting through clenched teeth 'That's for my boys' then he took off in the opposite direction.

It was so quick. It happened and was over in a few minutes. I rolled my sleeves all the way up and looked at my arms. I could see thin red marks but no bleeding. I calmly pushed myself up, told myself I was okay, put my headphones back in and continued walking home. When I got there, I removed my cardigan to wash my hands and face and noticed the cuts on my arms and hands had begun to bleed.

I sat in the bathroom on the edge of the bath and using a washcloth started to clean my wounds. I didn't use any soap but the cuts still stung. Once they were clean and dry I covered them in an antiseptic cream to stop any infection as I hadn't clearly seen what he used to cut me, and I covered my arms in a soft bandage.

I undressed, put on my pyjamas, and carefully got into bed. As I attempted to turn over, I suddenly felt a sharp twinge in my left shoulder, presumably from being thrown into the wall and I got out of bed. I swallowed a handful of different pain medication, not noticing or caring what I was taking, washed these down with a nice bottle of rose wine then went back to bed and tried with all my might to will myself to sleep but it didn't work.

In the morning I took the bandages off. I cleaned and dried the cuts again which were severely more noticeable by now and wondered how I would hide them in work. I decided the best thing to do was use plasters to cover the marks and got straight to accomplishing this. I had to use 12 plasters on my arms then hide these under a long-sleeved top for work. I would come up with some excuse on the spot if anyone asked me about the ones on my hands. I wasn't good at much but coming up with excuses on the spot was my speciality. I had decided against taking a shower as this would have stung and washed away the clotting blood which was currently stopping the bleeding.

My shoulder felt more uncomfortable than it did painful, like that feeling you have when you've slept funny on your arm. I checked it in the mirror and could see no evidence of bruising. My face was a little scratched and had slight bruising but I was a master at covering discolouration on my face so this did not cause me any worry. As I was brushing my hair, I felt a small lump at the back of my head but couldn't remember this being hit.

***

In total, my left wrist has been broken three times and my right wrist four. I've had cracked ribs, broken ribs, broken fingers, and knuckles; too many black eyes, cuts, and bruises to count. There is not one single part of my body that doesn't have a memory of what I've been through. Alex's most prize possession, other than his new trainers, was an old, rusted pocketknife. It had several different blades in it that all folded neatly inside the worn wooden handle. It wasn't very big, around ten centimetres when fully opened but it was rarely out of his hands. He would generally use it to cut into my skin, wave in front of my face if I wasn't doing something the way he wanted it to be done or tearing at my clothing if he didn't like what I was wearing that day.

When Alex said he was going to show up, he did. When Alex said something was going to happen, it did. Alex often planned while Dennis often acted on his emotions. In the beginning I used to fight back, I would scream and attempt to run but given time I recognised it easier and somewhat safer to just give up. If I weren't cowering or tensing my body then the beatings didn't feel as bad and they certainly didn't last as long. Sometimes Alex wouldn't put a finger on me, sometimes he would drive to my house and sit there in the car for hours. He didn't text or come to the door regardless of whether I was home alone or with someone. He just sat there and watched then drove off as though this was the most normal thing in the world to him.

Like clockwork the calls and messages started again. Unlike before I could not work out who was sending them this time. They never mentioned anything about the recent mini attack so I could only presume the messages were being sent by the same person who had acquired my number via Dennis, or his phone. Was he the same person who sent me those messages from Dennis's phone? I would never know.

All the messages hinted at something I needed to know but by this point I was disinterested and disheartened. After a week or so of this regular game of threats, I thought I had seen and heard it all. 'Could things really get any worse'? I tiredly asked myself.

'Sure it can' the Devil laughed.

I was sitting at home one night casually watching TV while painting my nails when I heard the familiar ding from my phone. I had been texting with a friend and thought nothing of it when I put my passcode in and opened the messages. There, staring back at me was the most horrifying message I had ever received. 'Gt a gr8 vid eh ye, wnty c it? Denny bhoy did ye gd. Poor wee dug didne dae any gd at a gard dug hidn ahun the bk eh the mtr' which translates to: Got a great video of you, want to see it? Dennis did you good. Poor little dog didn't do any good as a guard dog hiding behind the back of the car.

There had been several times throughout my life where I had felt chest pains, tingling in my hands and feet, heartbeat racing, palms sweating, ringing in the ears. However, I had never experienced panic like I did in this exact moment. Everything went dark. I felt weightless, like my whole body was floating, I was trying to grab at words, at sentences as they escaped me because nothing made sense. The silence growing, echoing in my head as I desperately tried to fight for my survival.

And just as it came, it went. I was eerily calm. Just as I had never felt panic like that, I had never felt calmness like this either. My heart was slow and steady, I could see clearly, the voices from the TV bringing me comfort. I felt safe, as if no harm could ever come to me. I looked down at my hands and they were steady. I stood up and my legs effortlessly carried me into the bathroom. I turned on the shower, undressed and got in. I had never in my life heard something quite as euphonious as the running water around me.

I got out and sat casually on the edge of the bed. Earlier that day I had been doing some crafting and left a pile of things on top of my dresser drawer. I gently looked up and saw the craft knife sitting on top of the pile. I nonchalantly got up and walked towards this before sitting down, moving the towel slightly to show my thigh and casually brought the knife down to my skin; one cut, two, three. I didn't feel anything as I sat there watching the blood escaping from the wound I had contrived. I felt no pain, no fear, no relief, nothing.

I tried to hurry my mind. I felt I should be panicking. I know I should have been feeling something but it were as though my senses had somehow or another been commutated off. I had never, not once in my whole life, ever thought about harming myself. I had enough people throughout the years doing it to me so why had I now done it to myself? I could not think of one single reason, and it didn't alarm me. Looking back now, I continue to feel unsteady, deplorable, and bitter. It was something I should never have done, a moment of weakness and despair on my part that I hope to never mirror.

As time went on, I tried to remember every single detail from that night but it were as though my mind was guarding me from something. I would only get snippets, never enough to paint a picture that could help me remember. The harder I pushed myself, the further from the memory I became. Had there been someone videoing what he did? There were only two other people there, the driver and the one playing with Max but had I missed someone? Was it one of those two? Was there a camera set up somewhere I hadn't seen? In the car? Outside? It had been dark, maybe I had missed something. I couldn't remember. But I knew if this were true, it would be the one thing to bring me down, to make me stop, to kill me. Even to this day I continue to live in fear of this videos existence.

I deleted the message, the first one I had ever deleted in twenty-one years then I blocked the number. I called my provided, paid the charge, and got my number changed again. It wasn't true. It *couldn't* be true.

Having something out in the world that could show such a gruesome moment, something someone else could see, how could I ever explain that away? It's built into me to justify by saying I tripped or fell, I wasn't being careful, always the clumsy one me, to act effectively well-adjusted but if this truly exists, would I survive it? Could I? Would I even want to? I hope that question remains unanswered throughout the remainder of my life.

Chapter Twenty-one

In the two years following the torturous message hinting at a video, I haven't heard from anyone. It's been radio silence. Recently things in my life had been challenging and a certain issue brought up similar feelings from my past. The current issue couldn't have been any further away from what happened before; however, the feelings were the same.

The feelings of being watched. Walking around with my headphones in, blasting music was the only way to calm my thoughts when alone. The flashbacks were intense, the nightmares too, they were incredibly life-like and I was beginning to battle the conflict of old familiar feelings creeping back into my life.

I went to work one morning after having no sleep at all, the flashbacks and feelings of terror had been vigorous during the night and I was drained. I knew deep down I couldn't handle much more and wondered when I would get a break.

My manager Olivia had always been exceptionally supportive towards me. On this morning she called me into her office to talk about something. As she spoke I sat there on the couch and I could hear her voice, her tone, could feel her watching me but inside I felt nothing. I sat looking out of the window; it was sunny but not yet warm and the only thought in my head was how I was going to end my life when I returned home that day. Not *if* I would, that decision had been made the moment I sat down and realised I had nothing left to lose. As we walked out of her office together she turned to me.

'Whatever you do, just don't go off sick. Promise me you won't go off sick' she pleaded. I knew sickness was slowly becoming an issue at work and she probably only worried about another number being added to the sickness list but I turned to her.

'I promise' I responded, barely above a whisper and said with no emotion. I survived my day and I returned home. I was physically and emotionally drained. I felt as though there was a force beneath me, hauling me down which became more intense with each step I took. I had already decided hours before I would use medication to aid me in ending my life.

I kept any sort of medication in a box within my bedroom, however, when I walked through my front door something unexpected happened. I walked up to the bedroom door, placed my hand on the handle and stopped. Olivia's words echoing in my head.

'Whatever you do, just don't go off sick. Promise me you won't go off sick'. I removed my hand, thinking of the promise I had made to return the next day. I warily walked into my living room where I softly sat down.

'I'll attend work tomorrow and follow through with my decision at the weekend' I firmly told myself. I sat there, motionless, hollow, and waited for darkness to come. When it did, I continued to sit there. I was too afraid of going into my bedroom as I knew I wasn't strong enough not to take a cocktail of medication. 'Whatever you do, just don't go off sick. Promise me you won't go off sick' played repeatedly in my mind all night. I had never broken a promise to anyone before and I wasn't about to let it be the last thing I did here on earth. So, I waited.

As the sun came up, I washed and dressed, using clothing that had been folded but not yet put away, still fearful of breaking my promise if I dared enter my bedroom, and I returned to work. I had no intention of doing anything purposeful that day but I did show up.

Olivia called me into her office, as she had done the day before, and asked me to sit down. She told me about this woman Dana who was part of a wellness group. Olivia explained that Dana had been incredibly supportive towards other staff and herself, and she casually asked me if I wanted to speak with her. Before she had finishing speaking I had already begun shaking my head no. Been there, done that, never going back. Talking with anyone never accomplished anything good. Olivia was not pushy; she did not force her opinions on me or tell me I had to see Dana. She was only informing me that she personally knew of this person who had helped and was asking if I wanted to speak with her. Simple as that.

As I left her office I concluded Olivia thought I were crazy and needed professional help. I sent a quick message to Tink and Lexi informing them of this and to my surprise, instead of responding telling me Olivia were nuts, they asked what did I have to lose by speaking with Dana? They told me it couldn't make anything worse and if Olivia was offering me this support then maybe I should, for once, not automatically dismiss it and instead reach out and take the help being offered to me. They continued by telling me they were so proud of me, something they had done, and repeatedly told me throughout our friendship.

I was dumfounded. Why had they agreed with Olivia? They didn't know her. They had never met her. I couldn't agree to see Dana as this would only show that I thought I were crazy too and the last thing I wanted was for my manager to think that of me. But as I stood there I thought back to my earlier conversation with Olivia, how she told me of Dana in such a positive way, sharing with me how she had helped others. Was this lies? Had she told me this in the hope it would help me say yes? I didn't think so. She looked sincere when she had spoken with me.

'Maybe I should do this' I encouraged myself. If not for me, at least for Olivia so she would see I weren't totally crazy. I walked slowly back to her office; the door was open and I knocked. She gestured for me to come in but I didn't.

'Can I change my mind and see Dana'? I asked.

'Absolutely' Olivia smiled. She didn't ask me to expand on my change in opinion or push me to talk anymore. I respected that. As I walked away I knew I had to conserve all the energy I had to fight against this Dana person and show her how fine I was so everyone would back off a little and I could complete my plan of ending my life.

About a week later I was busy working away at the computer when someone informed me Dana was here to see me. I knew she was coming; I had been counting down the days, gauging how much energy I had to accumulate daily to be ready to fight her, but I had been so engrossed in the work I was doing that day that I had completely lost track of time. I stood up and followed as we were guided to another room. I had been in this room many times before but only now were I noticing it had an inviting feel about it. There were three big double windows; these were usually opened as the room was warm and as I sat down I felt a refreshing flow of air dance across the back of my neck. The chair was comfortable with high sides and almost oval in shape. It was soft, the kind of softness that swallows you up and makes you feel welcome. The curtains, navy with silver slithers flowing through them, like a cascading waterfall. Three of the walls were painted a light grey, the feature wall papered with blues and greys, a mixture of hope and despair. As I sat there, I looked around the room, taking it all in and wondering if these were the walls that would finally hold the words to my deepest darkest secrets. I doubted it.

Dana introduced herself and told me about who she worked for, what her job was, went through the same script that professionals always do - about keeping everything confidential unless she thought I were a danger to myself or others. Therapists, counsellors, and mental health workers are like robots I thought, they're not able to start communicating with real people until they can say those opening lines in unison. I chuckled at this. If I were going to harm another, would I really come to her to discuss it first? The only two people in my life who had caused me great pain were dead. And as for myself, here I sat knowing I was ending my life, had the steps completed in my mind and she thought I would open up and tell her this within a few minutes of meeting her? She was clearly the crazy one and my feelings of sharing quickly crept back in.

As I sat there I studied Dana. She didn't look like a counsellor or therapist and she wasn't. She wasn't dressed in a tight stiff suit like the others had been, she was wearing jeans with a Marvel t-shirt and when I dared look at her, I noticed how her smile reached her eyes and didn't appear to be painted on and fake like the others before her. 'Don't let her fool you, she's just like the others' the voice in my head warned me.

'What are some of the things you need support with'? She started. I sat in silence. Where would I begin? How? I didn't respond. 'Okay, I've spoken with Olivia and she's extremely concerned about you, do you know why she would be concerned'? She gently fished for information. As I sat there, I realised I wasn't only exhausted I was angry, I was hurting, I was confused, I was done and I knew I couldn't handle much more. I was at my breaking point and it terrified me.

I looked at Dana and realised working with someone isn't something that is done easily, especially with the kind of madness I held bottled up in my head. The relationship had to feel just right in order for me to take that first step and open up. I smiled inside thinking 'Okay you think you can help me? You're not that good. Let's do this'. I ran hastily through almost everything that had happened in my life then sat back and waited on her working some magic. I had no faith in this working or in Dana's abilities and wasn't holding out any hope that things would change. But boy, was I about to find out just how wrong I could be.

Dana sat and listened tentatively to every word I said and I was surprised to notice she was not writing anything down. Had she already given up just by being introduced to me? Typical. I could see how this were going to go; I would have to spend the first ¾ of the next session, if there would even be one, going over everything I said in this one. Marvellous. Something else to waste my time with. Then another thought crept in, maybe she was genuinely listening to me? If she was, why? No-one else ever had. Was this her way of having me fall into a false sense of security? I couldn't risk that. I didn't have the time or patience to be played by someone new.

I remember clearly the first thing Dana gave to me after I hit her with my life story. It was validation. It was clear, unshakable, undeniable validation. She instantly validated it was okay, normal even, to feel the way I was feeling and to have the thoughts I did. I hadn't known this were something I even needed. This surprised me as no adult had ever given me clear validation like this before. It caught me off guard. Could she be different? Had Olivia been right about her? She had to be tested more before I could agree to that. 'I tried counselling once; the woman told me I had PTSD. I thought she was crazy; I left and never went back' I informed her. 'Ha, deal with that' the voice in my head yelled.

'I agree, you do have PTSD' she said without missing a beat. Before I could fight her on this, she went on to explain PTSD - it was a condition caused by a traumatic experience and included symptoms such as flashbacks, nightmares, feelings of anxiety and difficulty sleeping. I agreed that I did in fact suffer with that list of symptoms but that did not mean I had PTSD. When she asked why, I said PTSD was something that people returning from war or someone who had lived through something so unimaginably traumatic had. She sat there looking at me and agreed with this also and again told me this explanation was me. I had spent twenty-two years living through traumatic experiences and of course I would now have PTSD, how could I not?

I sat there lost in my own thoughts. No-one had ever explained it to me like that before. I was just a normal person; no-one special, I never thought something like that could have ever affected me. 'Maybe she is different' I thought. By the end of the session, not much had changed. I still felt the same as I had before I met her. I still thought it pointless and that she could never help me, but there was something new, something so small it was almost unrecognisable to me at first, something I thought was lost a long time ago and had long given up on ever feeling again. It was hope.

I made another appointment with Dana. As the sessions went on, I found myself opening up not because I was testing her, but because I was becoming comfortable around her and she was surprisingly easy to walk with. She never pushed me on anything I wasn't comfortable talking about and as I continued to open up she taught me realising I needed help and continuing to see her was a strength, not a weakness. She was extremely observant, reading between the lines and understanding my silences. She never made me feel as though my problems were less than. In that room with her, I began to feel safe.

Dana would offer advice and give tools to help me better control my thoughts and emotions. One of the things she asked me to do was change something; something big or something small but to change one thing each week which wouldn't seem like much at first but after a few weeks when I looked back, I would see all those little things had added up to something bigger, something better. Again, I thought this was silly but I was continuing to attend these sessions so Olivia wouldn't think I were completely crazy and instead think everything was fine so I went along with it.

One of my biggest things was having my phone on my person when in work. I constantly had it to hand in case anything bad happened or anyone needed me. There was a lot going on in my life at that time and I needed to be easily reachable.

A few days before, Olivia had asked me to keep my phone in my locker and not on me during work. 'Easy' I thought. This wasn't even a challenge and when Dana said about changing something each week, I thought this would be a good place to start. So, I came into work the next day, got changed and put my phone into my pocket. 'Nope, not today' I reminded myself. I placed the phone into my locker and started my shift. Within twenty minutes I started to notice how I had an unsettling feeling. Was something bad about to happen? I usually had a sense of feeling before something big happened, like I could smell it in the air, the hair on my arms and the back of my neck would stand to attention. I tried to push it to the back of my mind, went and got a bottle of water and continued working.

As the minutes painstakingly passed, I was feeling more and more agitated. After an hour or so I had a pounding headache and went to my locker for painkillers. I lifted up my phone to check for any messages and in that moment realised the uneasy feeling I had was not because something bad was going to happen, it was because I didn't have my phone on me. How ridiculous was that?!

I was almost hyperventilating because I didn't have my phone on me. I had to know straight away when anything happened so I could take a few moments to work out how to deal with it and pull myself together in order to show up and help everyone else. Constantly checking my messages was something that kept me relatively calm. If I had no messages, everything was fine and I was fine and there was nothing to worry about. Not having my phone, not being able to check whether everything was fine was causing me a lot of anxiety.

But I had said I would try to change something every week and had chosen this so I was going to do my best and stick to it, no matter how uncomfortable it made me feel. I knew my family had the contact number for work and if anything serious happened they would either call or show up so I had to push through this and realise it was not a big issue. By the end of the week, I felt calmer; nothing drastic had happened, everyone was as good as they could be and I was beginning to relax. I found it quite therapeutic to be able to lock my phone away, switch my brain off and get on with things.

Dana introduced me to two important things. One was an app called Insight Timer, and the other was a person named Brene Brown. The app was filled with mentoring, workshops, calming playlists, courses, and guided meditation. I mainly used the app when I went to bed and listened to a guided meditation for winding down and helping me sleep. I enjoyed this as you could set it to turn the app off when the meditation was done in case you had, in fact, fallen asleep which allowed me to drift off, not having to worry about turning my phone off when it was over. Now, at first, I was not a fan of this app, I didn't even like the sound of it when Dana was describing it to me. I had tried meditation before, but I was someone who could not sit still. I always had to be doing something, even if I were sitting watching TV, I had to be on my phone or tidying up, ironing, or on my laptop; I couldn't just sit still and watch TV. However, I had said I would look at it, and I'm glad I did. It took me a few nights to get used to. I didn't try it every night as I had very little faith in it, but the more I tried it, the more I found it did relax me even if it didn't always help me sleep, it did help me feel calmer.

The second thing was that being introduced to someone named Brene Brown changed my life through her work and not even in person. Dana had told me about a talk she had on a streaming service and shared how she thought it would be good for me. Again, I was not big on motivational speakers. I thought they were all filled with empty words and promises and couldn't help anyone, but I had finally settled down with not being in such close contact with my phone during the day. I was enjoying the app, so I thought 'why not watch this thing? What do I have to lose'? As it turned out, I had nothing to lose.

I watched the show, and I loved it. I googled her and found podcasts on a music app. I like things in my life to be in order, so instead of listening to the most recent podcast, I scrolled all the way to the bottom and started with the first one. Listening to these became like a drug to me. I had to listen to them every single day. They were filled with heartache, truth, laughter, strength, power, and they spoke directly to me. In all the podcasts, there was only one where I had to stop, take a step back, realise I was not okay, but it was okay to take a break from listening any further. I turned it off and went to bed, but as soon as I woke up the following day, I started it from the beginning and listened the whole way through. That podcast was labelled 'Tarana Burke and Brene Brown on Being Heard and Seen. This one glided through my walls like a knife through butter and pierced my very soul. It was so powerful and raw, and I was at a point in my life where I was ready for all it had to teach me. My mind was no longer stuck in the memory of my fourteen-year-old self.

I had never thought of myself as a strong person. Alex and Dennis were the reason I couldn't sleep all these years later, and why I continue to have nightmares and flashbacks. Things happened, and I had two choices. I could either give up or keep going. It was that simple. My choices were simple, yes; however, keeping it going was the most difficult thing to do. My coping methods had not always been the best, or even legal, but they had gotten me this far in my life, so could they really have been that bad? Had my fear kept me safe, or too safe? Holding onto my memories was like holding onto glass too firmly; it would slit my hands too deeply.

If someone asked me how I've done this for so long, I wouldn't be able to give them an answer. I honestly don't know. A day turns into a week, turns into a month, and before you know it, twenty years have passed. I know that sounds crazy, but it is really crazy. It hasn't been constant; I did have breaks, and maybe that's what kept me going, that it didn't all completely stop, and then I had to deal with it. I don't understand why I'm still alive; how had I survived after everything that had happened? Was I always meant to live? I have spent my life pushing people away, friends who were worried, teachers who thought they knew better, police who could have helped, and colleagues who had to stand by and watch me struggle through yet another beating. I'm tired of pushing people away; maybe it's time to start trusting people. I have to remind myself not everyone is like Alex and Dennis; there is good in this world.

From that awful night when this all started until I were twenty-five years old, I had only told three people. My best friend who cried, my mother who acted like I had done her wrong, and my teacher who offered no support. After eleven years, I was tired and tried to open up more, but counselling brought me no comfort, speaking with people online made me feel good and feel as though I could help others, but it took its toll on me. It wasn't until I met Tink and Lexi that I finally realised it was okay to open up, safe even. It wasn't until I had a manager who made an off-the-cuff remark about not going off sick did I realise I could survive one more day. And it wasn't until I started speaking with someone did I realise I was not okay, and that was okay.

I was looking online one day and found this quote - 'Unlearning abuse also means unlearning the abusive behaviours that you inherited as survival tactics'. It hit me. It made complete sense. Trouble and the behaviours I inherited have made me who I am; this has been over twenty years of my life. I don't know who I am without this, so what do I do now? It's hard to bury your past. Alex and Dennis had ruined me; they had taken so much from me. I had met evil as a child, and it had entangled itself throughout my life. Every time I stood in front of a mirror, I saw the ghost of the child I once was.

But with the tools and belief I now had in myself, I was more determined than even that I would survive this and get my life back. They'll watch as I set the world on fire. 'I'll show you how a princess fights' I said out loud to Alex, hoping that wherever he was, he would hear me. 'I'm not that kid you left to die'.

In the end, I realised talking with someone was the best thing I had ever done. Talk therapy had helped me put structure and organisation to my thoughts and feelings. It had soothed me, reducing accoutrements of the detrimental saga my lives betrayals had held over me all these years.

When someone is physically beaten you see the damage on their skin, you can watch how it heals overtime. My body was painted with scars from my battles, a roadmap of my horrors. What you cannot see is the damage those same beatings caused on my brain and heart, and this takes far longer to heal than bruising does. This type of damage cannot easily be covered up or explained away, it requires years of healing. But I refuse to let it break me anymore. After everything I have been through, it has only resulted in making me stronger.

That room, and Dana, had become my safe space. A cocoon if you like, where I was finally allowing myself permission to repair what had been broken all those years before. I wanted to become a whole person again and not just the cracked shadow that I had painstakingly become. I wanted to live and not just survive. I was finally allowing myself permission to be vulnerable and to heal.

THE END

Printed in Great Britain
by Amazon